Minimum Wages in Central and Eastern Europe:
from protection to destitution

Minimum Wages in Central and Eastern Europe: from protection to destitution

EDITED BY

Guy Standing and
Daniel Vaughan-Whitehead

MCK
HD
4921
.C4 M5
1995

Prepared by The International Labour Office
Central and Eastern European Team (ILO-CEET)
Budapest

CEU

Central European University Press
BUDAPEST   LONDON   NEW YORK

This edition first published 1995 by the Central European University Press,
H-1051 Budapest, Nádor utca 9, Hungary,
in association with
ILO Central and Eastern European Multidisciplinary Advisory Team (CEET),
ILO-CEET, H-1066 Budapest, Mozsár utca 14, Hungary

Distributed by
Oxford University Press, Walton Street, Oxford OX2 6DP
Oxford New York Athens Auckland Bangkok Bombay Toronto
Calcutta Cape Town Dar es Salaam Delhi Florence Hong Kong
Istanbul Karachi Kuala Lumpur Madras Madrid Melbourne
Mexico City Nairobi Paris Singapore Taipei Tokyo Toronto
and associated companies in Berlin Ibadan
Distributed in the United States
by Oxford University Press Inc., New York

ISBN: 1 85866 042 4 Hbk
ISBN: 1 85866 043 2 Pbk

Typeset by James Patterson
Printed and bound in Great Britain by Redwood Books

Contents

List of Tables and Figures

Chapter 5

Chapter 6

Chapter 7

Introduction

Guy Standing and Daniel Vaughan–Whitehead

The statutory minimum wage has long been a source of intense political and economic controversy. Seen by many as the ultimate source of social protection against exploitation and poverty, it has been seen by generations of critics as a 'market distortion', pricing workers out of jobs and denying the freedom of employment contracts.

In the countries of Central and Eastern Europe, the minimum wage was a key variable in the wage system operating under the command economy, and there is little doubt that it acted as an effective floor for the wage tariff and a barrier to severe poverty, even though average wages were close to the minimum wage. And both were low, in part because of the high ratio of non–wage to wage remuneration, and in part simply because wages and productivity were remarkably low.

The trouble was that the way the minimum wage was set or used under the former system was inappropriate for a market–oriented economy, and subsequent events demonstrated that it was not adapted to meet the extraordinary crises into which the emerging labour markets of the region were plunged. Tragically, for millions of workers and their families, the minimum wage became a means by which their impoverishment was intensified. This is the main claim underlying and justifying this book.

The minimum wage as a policy instrument has been more important, or instrumental, in Central and Eastern Europe than elsewhere, yet it has received surprisingly little attention in the extensive debates about the reform strategies in the region. This was why the ILO's Central and Eastern European Team decided to launch a series of analyses of how the minimum wage has evolved since 1989 in countries of the region. Most of the resultant studies are included in this volume, prepared mainly by economists from the countries concerned. As such, they have emphasised different aspects that they regarded as having most priority in their countries.

There are some common threads, as was intended. Although there is also a series of specific issues, mainly concerned with the potential effects on wages and employment, the most serious general theme is that, with the partial exception of Poland, the Czech Republic and Slovakia the minimum wage has been allowed or encouraged to fall to terribly low levels, well below any sensible level of subsistence income.   In most countries, the minimum wage fell to a small fraction of the average wage, and in this respect there are considerable differences between the countries of Central and Eastern Europe and Western Europe. Typically, in the latter the minimum wage has been about two–thirds of the average.[1]

Let us be clear that what we are considering is a statutory minimum wage, that is, a wage rate below which employers in normal or predetermined circumstances may not employ workers. This is what the International Labour Office has promoted for many decades.[2] This should be distinguished from a negotiated minimum wage that is determined by means of collective bargaining on behalf of contracting parties, the employer and workers. But therein lies a problem, since in some countries it is also true that the statutory minimum wage is subject to determinedly tripartite bargaining at the national level, and in some cases at the industry level or even regional level.

The crucial point is that there should be a law and a derived set of procedures by which the statutory minimum is determined. Normally, the legislation and procedures should also determine the mechanisms and institutions for monitoring adherence and for adjusting the minimum to ensure that its value is acceptable and that its coverage is consistent with the legislative objectives.

In all these respects, there has been cause for considerable concern in most countries of Central and Eastern Europe. A basic conclusion and recommendation of this book is that a great deal could and should be done to make minimum wage fixing, implementation and monitoring more effective in these countries. Above all, as brought out in most of the following chapters, there is an urgent need to enhance and then to preserve the real value of the minimum wage, if it is intended to be a desirable policy instrument. Few if any countries have developed satisfactorily the institutional machinery for achieving those objectives.

There are those, of course, who believe fervently that the statutory minimum wage should be removed from the armoury of labour market regulations. We believe that view is at best too strong, and that there is not the empirical evidence to justify that strong policy conclusion. There are many claims to

[1]   Institute of Personnel Management: *Minimum Wage: An Analysis of the Issues* (London, IPM, 1991).

[2]   See, for instance, International Labour Organisation: *Minimum Wages: Wage Fixing Machinery. Application and Supervision*, Geneva, ILO Conference, 79th Session, 1992.

that effect, yet as long as there is an absence of evidence to support them—as Chapters 2 and 10 argue—then surely there should be an a priori presumption that it is better to have an instrument to protect the low–paid from destitution than to dispense with it, and that if the authorities have such an instrument those authorities should do what they can to see that it is utilised properly and fairly.

There are also those who feel that the statutory minimum wage should be something to which one pays 'lip service' while allowing it to fall steadily into disuse until such time as it could be quietly abandoned. This view should be deplored. If put into practice, it could have adverse consequences for policy implementation on a broader scale, spreading an ethos of bureau-cratic cynicism that is likely to result in administrative inefficiency.

Yet this leaves the issue in awkward territory. Does a minimum wage actually protect the low–paid, and can it protect them in the more flex-ible labour markets emerging in Central and Eastern Europe and elsewhere? This issue is taken up in different ways in Chapters 1 and 2. We believe that the minimum wage has had declining significance and impact, both actual and potential, and that it needs to be supplemented by other instruments more than ever before. However, that in no way should be interpreted as suggesting that we would wish to see the mini-mum wage removed. Above all, it should be a standard for decency in the labour market.

One argument, reiterated by the World Bank's report to the global *Social Summit*, is that because the minimum wage has fallen relative to other sources of income, it is unimportant. One appreciates the point that in such circumstances it should not be seen as a major distorting phenomenon, yet the cause and effect could easily be mixed. Those adherents of the minimum wage could retort that it is because the mini-mum wage has been neglected that it has shrunk as a share of average earnings, and that it is because of this that it is important to raise it and develop the procedures to ensure its value.

The papers in this book examine various aspects of the minimum wage in Central and Eastern Europe. Before doing so, Chapter 1 discusses the role of the minimum wage more generally in terms of whether or not it remains an effective instrument for securing distributive justice. Chapter 2 presents a comparative analysis of minimum wage trends in the countries of Central and Eastern Europe, showing that it no longer constitutes an anchor for social protection and that, deliberately or otherwise, it has become an instrument for controlling wage growth.

Chapter 3 shows how the minimum wage in the Russian Federation has fallen well below any conceivable definition of the poverty line. It proposes that for such a vast country, with considerable variations in prices and living standards between regions, a regionalised approach to establish negotiated minimum wages would be preferable to, or complement the establishment of a single rate for the whole country. One of the biggest problems is the discrepancy in average earnings between the privatised and the public service sectors in the country. It has been a feature of the Russian labour market that wages in the public 'budgetary' sector have lagged well behind the average in the rest of the economy, and the minimum wage has not been useful in protecting the living standards of many groups in public services.

Chapter 4 shows that in Poland as well, the minimum wage has been used to control overall wage growth. But unlike the situation in the Russian Federation the level of social benefits was disconnected from the minimum wage and an indexation system has been introduced. As a result, Poland has been the only country in the region in which the minimum wage increased relative to the average wage.

Chapter 5 highlights how the minimum wage has been determined by tripartite negotiations in Hungary, within the aptly named National Council for the Reconciliation of Interests. It is noteworthy that the negotiations were made easier when the Government decided to drop its version of a tax–based incomes policy in 1993. So too is the fact that the Hungarian experience illustrates how the minimum wage could play a role in developing collective bargaining on wages. What should not be forgotten is that the minimum wage has remained well below the officially recognised subsistence income, and the anticipated increase in the price of energy may erode the real value even further. Moreover, there has been a consistent problem arising from a lack of enforcement of the minimum wage. In 1992, for instance, official data indicated that over one–quarter of all workers were receiving below the minimum wage, in part because many enterprises were apparently unable to pay wages of that level. As a result, some sectoral level minimum wage bargaining has emerged, with some sectors, such as agriculture, paying less than the official national minimum wage. It will be important for national policymakers in Hungary and in other countries of the region to monitor this disaggregated approach.

Chapter 6 describes the trends in the minimum and average wages in the Czech Republic, but concentrates mostly on an assessment of the possible effects of an increase in the minimum wage in January 1992 on wages and employment. Perhaps it was not surprising that the modest increase had no appreciable effect; what was perhaps more surprising was that the low minimum wage was left unchanged throughout the prolonged period covered by the analysis. Although the minimum wage in the Czech Republic covered only a very small proportion of the national workforce, the numbers in a few sectors were more substantial.

Chapter 7 shows that in Bulgaria the minimum wage fell in real terms by an enormous amount, even more than average wages. The main reason was that the Tripartite Committee, which set the minimum wage, was suspended in 1991–92, so that it was left unchanged in money terms for almost two years, during which there was a massive price inflation. This also reflected the stabilisation policy pursued by the Government, pressed by the IMF and the World Bank, which was associated with a substantial rise in poverty and in the number of unemployed and workers on very low wages.

The Bulgarian experience highlights the need for an indexation system of some kind (in fact introduced in 1993) in a period of high inflation, if the minimum wage is to be a meaningful anchor of social protection. Another feature highlighted by the Bulgarian experience is that those receiving about the minimum wage tend to be concentrated in a few sectors, and thus those concerned with assuring its implementation should be encouraged to focus on those sectors. In the case of Bulgaria, there is considerable evidence that a very large number of workers have been paid well below the minimum wage.

Chapter 8 shows how the minimum wage in Romania fell in real terms and in relation to the average wage and to the subsistence income. But the minimum wage has played an important role in determining the whole wage structure, since the wage at industry or sectoral level has been determined on the basis of coefficients multiplied by the minimum wage. A consequent contrast with some other countries in the region, such as Bulgaria and the Czech Republic, where the minimum wage has not had much effect on average wages, is that in Romania it has had an automatic effect on wage differentials. Before the national minimum wage in Romania could be raised to a level capable of meeting basic subsistence needs, it would seem essential to reform the wage determination process. In any case, that would mean sectoral wage differentials being allowed to adjust to reflect economic conditions to a greater extent than has evidently been the case.

In the Republic of Moldova, as Chapter 9 shows, the minimum wage fell dramatically below the subsistence level of income. This was due primarily to a very centralised wage system involving wage fund controls and the nonimplementation of the *Law on wage indexation of December 1991*. The Republic of Moldova is like other countries where the so–called 'transition' period has brought a substantial deterioration in living standards among the low paid, which means a large proportion of the population.

Finally, Chapter 10 returns to developments in the minimum wage in Western Europe, the main message being that there has not been any convincing empirical evidence showing that the minimum wage has had the predicted effect on employment.

Since these papers were prepared, the OECD has published its *Jobs Study* and background papers. A strong attack is made on the minimum wage as an instrument for labour market regulation. Yet the report is very selective of the studies it cites, and overlooks studies that have indicated that the adverse effect on employment is minimal or nonexistent.[3] We have little doubt that the strong claims made about the effects of the minimum wage are exaggerated, and that the most important positive contribution minimum wages can play—if set properly to protect the low–paid from absolute poverty—is to set standards of decency.

These papers represent the evolving state of the art on debates on wages in what is a rapidly evolving labour market in the countries of the region. It is hoped that they will encourage others to probe many of the issues touched in the course of the analyses. In their preparation, we have had kind assistance from colleagues in Budapest, Geneva and elsewhere. In particular, we would like to thank Gilbert Benhayoun and Stephen Bazen for organising an important conference on minimum wages and low pay in Arles, France in September 1993, giving us the opportunity to set up this group of experts; and James Patterson who carried out both the copy editing and the typesetting.

---

[3] See, for example, D. Card: 'Do minimum wage laws reduce employment? A case study of California, 1987–89', in *Industrial and Labour Relations Review*, Vol. 46, No. 1, Oct. 1992, pp. 39–54.

1

What Role for the Minimum Wage in the Flexible Labour Markets of the 21st Century?

Guy Standing*

1. Introduction

In Central and Eastern Europe and elsewhere, mass unemployment and rising poverty and inequality raise questions about the efficacy of traditional systems of remuneration and income support. Quite right too. Internationally, there has been much debate about abolition of the statutory minimum wage. The main argument of this and related papers is that in Central and Eastern Europe the roles of the minimum wage should be revised and that politicians, economists and social policy specialists should not be led to US–style 'social safety net' versions of social protection.

Two themes should be stressed. Arguments for retention of minimum wages are not so much right or wrong as of declining significance. And, as used in Central and Eastern Europe, the minimum wage has actually become a means of impoverishment. This could and should be stopped without delay.

The ILO Central and Eastern European Team has been conducting studies of the role of minimum wages in countries of the region, with the following conclusions. First, the value of minimum wages has fallen sharply relative to average wages, which in most cases have also fallen in real terms. The relative decline has occurred in all countries with the exception of Poland. Second, the minimum wage has fallen well below the subsistence income level in all countries; the most extreme case is Ukraine. Third, the minimum wage has been used as an instrument for setting social protection benefits, so perversely because of that it has been used as a means of controlling social expenditure. For example, in Russia unemployment benefits are supposed to be earnings related, with a base set by the minimum wage. Because of rapid inflation and delays in attaining entitlement to benefits, those actually receiving unemployment benefits have been receiving the minimum wage amount. Because the minimum wage is only adjusted periodically by decree, it has lagged well behind inflation and average money wages, and thus the minimum wage has

* ILO, Labour Market Policies Branch, Geneva.

become a means by which the unemployed, pensioners and low–paid workers have become impoverished.

Similar links exist elsewhere, and in some countries external advisers and international institutions have encouraged governments to maintain the monetary value of the minimum wage as an anti–inflationary device, despite galloping inflation. Meanwhile, although few workers in employment receive the minimum wage in most countries, it is still widely used for wage tariff purposes and for determining what should be paid to workers on 'unpaid' or 'partially paid' leave. In sum, its role is still substantial.

We strongly recommend that the link between the minimum wage and social benefits be broken. Benefit levels should be determined by subsistence needs and perhaps have earnings–related supplements, whereas the minimum wage should be determined by tripartite bargaining, taking account of income needs, productivity criteria and labour market factors.

What should be the future role of statutory minimum wages? They should not be abolished, although the arguments for their retention are weakening. One can refute the traditional arguments against them as theoretically and empirically flawed.[1]

Critics of minimum wages usually claim that they push the wage above the 'market clearing' level and thus cause high unemployment.[2] More elaborate variants include a belief that they raise the whole structure of wages. One can answer these claims by referring to efficiency wage theory, productivity effects and the lack of evidence that statutory minimum wages do raise unemployment. In spite of claims by the OECD in its *Jobs Study* that minimum wages lower employment, the empirical studies in North America and Western Europe have not shown large or consistent effects, and those pointing to the absence of an effect—as well as some suggesting a *positive* effect—were conveniently overlooked in the OECD Study.[3] At best, one should be eclectic about the effects on employment and unemployment. There must be a strong probability that many employers could find ways round the minimum wage if it seriously affected their possibility of employing labour.

Increasingly, workers who need the sort of income protection sought through statutory minimum wages are not stuck in mills or large–scale

[1] For this writer's elaboration of this argument, see G. Standing: 'Structural adjustment and labour market policies', in G. Standing and V. Tokman (eds.): *Towards Social Adjustment? Labour Market Policies in Structural Adjustment* (Geneva, ILO, 1991), pp. 5–52.

[2] For an example of a recent restatement, see 'Rich man, poor man', in *The Economist* (London), 24 July 1993, p. 65, citing the latest OECD *Employment Outlook.*.

[3] For an example of a study that found a substantial positive effect on employment of a rise in the minimum wage, see L. Katz and A. Krueger: 'The effect of the minimum wage on the fast food industry', in *Industrial and Labour Relations Review*, Vol. 46, No. 1, October 1992, pp. 6–21. For a study of the impact of the minimum wage in Greece that found only a small effect on employment, see V. Koutsogeorgopoulou: 'The impact of minimum wages on industrial wages and employment in Greece', in *International Journal of Manpower*, Vol. 15, Nos. 2/3, 1994, pp. 86–99.

factories. They are doing part–time work in domestic or consumer services; they are homeworkers doing piece work; they are on the periphery, the 'flexiworkers' who have to spin out their working lives through odd jobs, casual labour and the like.

A statutory regulatory apparatus is unsuited for those situations. The high probability that such work is in the black, shadow or informal economy—or that part of the payment is 'under the table'—means there is likely to be a fear or reticence on the part of the workers to giving information that might implicate them in illegality or expose them to retribution. The probability is high that they will not be paying employee contributions or self–employed contributions to social security, or be taking account of all the income they earn in applying for means–tested benefits. The fact that in most cases were they to reveal the little income they receive would mean no difference to their entitlement does not alter the reality that the working poor lack the voice or sense of security to exercise their rights.

2. Arguments for a Minimum Wage

Let us briefly consider the arguments in favour of the minimum wage in the light of the labour insecurity characteristic of the 'flexible' labour markets of the 1990s.

First, traditionally it has been promoted as an instrument for *preventing and reducing poverty*. The trouble is that it is increasingly inefficient, because most of the poor in modern societies are outside regular wage employment and in part because, however you measure the minimum wage (hourly, weekly, monthly), the difference between money income and the level of full income required to raise a person above the poverty line has been growing. The minimum wage cannot provide low–paid workers with income security effectively, because it cannot reach most of those who need it and because the wage share of total remuneration has fallen so much.

Second, it is a mechanism for integrating the low–paid into the labour force. Increasingly, collective mechanisms are bypassed by the individualisation and *contractualisation* of labour relations. Labour markets are moving from being based on collective or 'team' contracts to being based on individual contracts. If one accepts that as a reality, however one might feel about it, one should recognise that the trend erodes the regulatory potential of statutory minimum wages.

Third, it may have a *demonstration effect* by setting decency thresholds for wages, leading employers to set higher wages even though they are under no regulatory pressure to do so. For this to be anything more than a gesture requires the minimum wage to be socially legitimised and applicable to a sufficient number of workers who would be in poverty without it. If most workers perceive that they are not affected by the minimum wage, its demonstration effect will be minimised. How many workers would take to the barricades in defence of the minimum wage?

Fourth, a minimum wage is intended to *combat 'sweating'*, i.e. limiting pressure on workers to work excessively long in order to achieve a minimal subsistence income. But when the monthly minimum wage is set as the statutory instrument, what is to control working time or work intensity or the implicit 'contract' between employer and worker by which certain tasks have to be done in addition to those covered in the formal working week? As more of the working poor are outside factory or office blocks, what is to protect them from sweating? There are many reasons deterring such workers from protesting against sweating, notably fear of dismissal, loss of income and difficulty of proving the case.

Fifth, a statutory minimum wage may be defended as a means of *boosting productivity* and efficiency. This argument relates to the 'efficiency wage' hypothesis—a worker who has sufficient income to be able to afford adequate food, clothing, etc. can work more efficiently—and to what one might call the 'effort bargain' of the employment relationship.[4] This argument is surely correct, but probably it does not go very far. A reasonable minimum wage may boost efficiency and the effort of some workers, but there are better ways of doing that, including incentive–based payment systems.

Sixth, it is believed that statutory minimum wages stimulate productivity more generally by *inducing technological change* and by inducing skill upgrading by checking the resort to low–wage, cheap labour production strategies. This argument is usually overlooked by critics of the minimum wage.[5] However, it is of diminishing importance in the modern high–tech production systems of the 1990s, in which wage costs as a share of production costs are so low that small changes in the wage rates of the low–skilled would not induce much reaction.

Seventh, defenders of minimum wages argue that they *reduce income inequality*, because they lead to a compression of wage differentials higher up the wage ladder. To the extent that they do so, they may lead firms to opt for more training to raise the supply of high–skilled workers. All well and good, if that is empirically supported, although many neoclassical

---

[4] In Central and Eastern Europe, this is linked to the well–known adage, 'They pretend to pay us, we pretend to work.' There is also interesting material in Western Europe on links between workers being remunerated below what is perceived to be a 'just wage' and their resort to sabotage, larceny and loitering.

[5] The popular view that the USA's 'jobs miracle' (sic) is due to the relative lack of wage and employment regulations and low non–wage labour costs by contrast with those in Western Europe should always prompt reminders to its advocates that this was combined with dismal levels of productivity growth in the 1980s, which contributed to the huge budget and trade deficits.

labour economists believe wage differentials should increase so as to help the low–skilled find employment. However, the more flexible labour relations situation of the 1990s erodes the relevance of this argument. For many groups the wage is a diminishing part of total remuneration, and probably over a fairly wide range the ratio of non–wage to wage remuneration rises the higher the income category of employee.

Raising the minimum wage may lead to a shift towards money wages for lower–paid groups, and a cut in other forms of 'remuneration', including training. Decentralisation of wage bargaining also probably means that raising the minimum wage would have little effect on wages higher up the scale because such structures are increasingly things of the past, and will certainly become so in Central and Eastern Europe soon.

Eighth, the minimum wage provides an *anchor for social transfers* and the system of social protection. This has been one of its major roles in Central and Eastern Europe.[6] The quicker the link is broken the better.

In a situation of high unemployment, more flexible labour markets and informalisation of the economy, the social budget has been targeted for cuts everywhere. Where is there a government that has resisted this pressure? When confronted with a choice between that and protecting a small minority of low–paid workers, governments can rationalise concentrating on reducing public expenditure by holding down the minimum wage as a relatively easy means of limiting public transfers, as was done in Bulgaria in 1992. We may deplore this tendency, but it is an awkward political reality. The minimum wage should be set by reference to social productivity; the income levels for social protection should be linked to the need to prevent poverty and social deprivation in the economic and social conditions of the country at the time.

Ninth, there is the argument that the minimum wage is efficient because it is *administratively simple.* This simplicity is all right as long as you do not expect too much of it. Workers paid less than the minimum are supposed to be in an easy position to report violations. Yet in practice, most would have neither the voice nor the social strength to do so. Moreover, because of administrative difficulties, many governments have exempted certain types of employment from coverage by statutory minimum wages—such as part–timers in the Netherlands, casual labour in Belgium, and those working in small–scale businesses in the USA and elsewhere. Yet those not covered comprise many of the lowest–paid groups in the flexible, informal labour markets that are fast emerging.

In sum, although the traditional arguments for championing a statutory minimum wage remain, they are of diminishing relevance as European labour

---

[6] See Chapters 2 and 3.

markets evolve towards a very different model than when the minimum wage was the anchor of working class aspirations in industrial society.

If one is serious about protecting the low–paid and working poor, and about reducing exploitation in modern European societies, something more radical and comprehensive than the statutory minimum wage will probably be needed. Several specialists have, for instance, proposed a more 'universal' social protection system and a move towards a Citizenship Income Guarantee, paid to each individual as a right of citizenship, regardless of work or wage—earning status, employment record, marital status, age or gender. Bear in mind the greater poverty and income inequality, the erosion of entitlement to income protection and the problems of low *take–up* of means–tested selective transfers. This has produced an unsavoury spread of social detachment, anomie and deprivation. Measures such as minimum wages were meant as instruments for social solidarity, for integrating the vulnerable into a society of common human dignity, as instruments for citizenship. Given what has happened to poverty and inequality, one must realise that one is tinkering with a very small part of the engine and that too much is left out of the tinkering to make it worth a lot of debate.

3. A Drift to Workfare?

Underlying the failure to protect low–income groups from deprivation and poverty in Western Europe and North America is the erosion of a basic premise of the post–1945 welfare state. Income support in industrial society was supposed to imply entitlement to compensation for 'temporary interruption of earning power' and for retirement.

That was based on a model of *social insurance*, in which the individual's risk of need for income to compensate for illness, disability, unemployment and so on was collectivised. Social insurance has its roots in the nineteenth century, and many would argue that it originated as a means of preserving social stability and social stratification.[7] But in the course of the twentieth century, particularly since the Second World War, it has been extended to embrace more diverse forms of risk and economic need, which helped put it under increasing strain. The predominant post–1945 model presumed 'full employment' and a labour force in steady, full–time jobs, as well as a social structure based on a nuclear family and a 'male breadwinner', who was supposed to have a long period of working life followed by a short period in income–insured retirement. Without those premises, there was a tendency

---

[7] See, for instance, G. Esping Andersen: *The Three Worlds of Welfare Capitalism* (Princeton, Princeton University Press, 1990).

for contributions to fail to match benefit requirements. Yet all those premises have long been weakened, and some were never valid.

Millions of people are cut off from regular full–time employment, whether in part–time or casual jobs, in long–term unemployment, or in 'underclass' survival activities. Both the contributory base and the entitlements' base have been eroded. The loss of legitimacy of the welfare system is leading to 'workfare' (obliging people to take low–paid work in return for benefits). It is coming little by little—a condition for benefit entitlement tightened here, another there, a new definition introduced here and there, and so on. In most countries, only a minority of the unemployed receive unemployment benefits, and a host of conditions have been introduced to limit access to other benefits. Now, similar procedures and benefits are being introduced in Central and Eastern Europe, with disastrous consequences.

While minimum wage machinery has become less efficient and meaningful in the more flexible labour markets, so there has been *explicit disentitlement* to state–based income support, through a tightening of regulations, and *implicit disentitlement,* through more people finding themselves in work statuses and with work histories that prevent them from having access to benefits.

Meanwhile, governments have been moving in the direction of trying to re–regulate the behaviour of the poor, some with the best of intentions, some with more questionable motives. So–called '*active*' labour market and social policy may conjure up an image of enabling the poor and marginalised to be reintegrated into the economic mainstream, but it could become a euphemism for schemes to turn the poor into *passive* clients of government regulation.

In the USA, President Bill Clinton has stated that his administration intends to 'end welfare as we know it'. Workfare is firmly at the centre of reformist thinking, just as many of its elements are in Europe. The trend to workfare relates to the relevance and potential of statutory minimum wages, and should not be excluded from debates on it.

The rhetoric of workfare has overtones of coercion and regulation behind the commitment to 'participation' and 'reintegration'. It resurrects such dubious notions as the 'deserving' and 'undeserving poor', and leads to differentiating between the 'employable' and the 'unemployable' (e.g. women with babies).

Workfare schemes, whether couched in terms of the US debates or in terms of Active Labour Market Policy, must invite concern about *substitution effects* at the bottom of the labour market, and about undermining the fragile effectiveness of minimum wages.[8] Ironically, the strongest

---

[8] Such effects were found in the workfare experiments in San Diego, California, in the 1980s.

advocates of workfare are typically the libertarian New Right, who place a high premium on the 'right to choose'. Yet workfare involves limiting that freedom for the poor and obliging them to take jobs or 'training' for wages that are at or below the level of the minimum wage.[9] Indeed, one argument made for workfare is that it would lower wages at the lower end of the spectrum and thus lead to increased demand for low–skilled labour. This is an unattractive argument.

4. Conclusion

Debates about the minimum wage are ultimately about distributive justice. After more than a decade during which distributional issues were marginalised, there is a renewed sense of concern. Perhaps a new set of terms and ways of thinking must come with that. One misleading euphemism of the past decade is 'deregulation', when in fact there has been a drift from pro–collective regulations to pro–individualistic regulations. In the next decade, debates about redistribution will have to build on the emerging realities of flexible labour markets, flexible payment systems, individualised employment contracts, part–time working, subcontracting, 'occupational multiplicity' and the informal economy.

A statutory minimum wage is relatively suitable for an economy in which the vast majority of the workforce are in regular, full–time employment, and where unions are pervasive. Yet what should the minimum wage be if half the workforce work variable hours in a mixture of wage and own–account work, when one month you will earn practically nothing on the implicit understanding that in another month you will earn substantial profit–related pay? What happens to the man or woman who helps a friend with a local business to give himself a supplementary income, and as a result that friend reduces the working hours of his assistant to the point where it falls short of the minimum wage?

One could multiply the examples many times. Instances of this type are likely to be typical of the more flexible productive and labour market systems that are emerging all over the world. Will we still be debating the merits and demerits of statutory minimum wages in ten years time? It seems unlikely. For the present, let us put them in their proper place, to protect the poor, not impoverish the victims of structural adjustment.

---

[9] The writer has tried to review the arguments for and against workfare elsewhere. G. Standing: 'The road to workfare: Alternative to welfare or threat to occupation?', in *International Labour Review*, Vol. 129, No. 6, 1990, pp. 677–91.

2

Minimum Wages in Central and Eastern Europe: Slippage of the Anchor

Daniel Vaughan–Whitehead*

1. Introduction

In the current transition period we could have expected minimum wages to play an important role. First, they could be expected to protect the lowest paid and most vulnerable workers and try to maintain their minimum physical and social needs from an emerging, imperfect labour market. Second, by representing the base of the total wage hierarchy they could have been expected to constitute a potentially important variable of macro economic adjustment. Third, after a period dominated by low wages and full employment, they could be expected to oblige enterprises to improve labour productivity and accelerate their restructuring rather than pursue a low wage policy. Finally, they could be expected to offer an instrument for promoting collective bargaining between the state on one side and trade unions and employers' representatives on the other. However, reality after over four years of reform is rather different. Although governments in most of the countries of the region have introduced or maintained national minimum wages, they have not played their expected social and economic roles.

In a context of economic decline, collapse of external and domestic markets and price liberalisation, most governments implemented a restrictive tax–based incomes policy, as advocated by the IMF and the World Bank, and tried to use a statutory minimum wage to control labour costs and keep inflation under control, considering the minimum wage more as a source of distortions than a crucial social and economic instrument.[1] This

* ILO Central and Eastern European Team, Budapest. I am grateful to Alena Buchtikova, Tatyana Chetvernina, Krzystof Hagemejer, Jenő Koltay, and Guy Standing for their comments and suggestions. Thanks for providing data are also due to Diana Metohu (Ministry of Labour, Albania), Mia Lokk (Estonian Trade Union Research and Development Centre), Ewa Tomaszewska, Elzbieta Urbanowicz (Solidarnosc) and Stefan Skledar (Confederation of New Trade Unions of Slovenia).
[1] 'Labour market policies—minimum wages, job security regulations, and social security—are usually intended to raise welfare or reduce exploitation. But they actually work to raise the cost of labour in the formal sector and reduce labour demand ... increase the supply of labour to the rural and urban informal sectors, and thus depress labour incomes where most of the poor are found': *The Challenge of Development*, World Bank Development Report, p. 63 (Washington DC, World Bank, 1991).

paper analyses the adverse effects of this policy, before identifying some of the changes that could be introduced to improve the minimum wage fixing process.

2. Downward Pressure on Minimum Wages

The policy of price liberalisation launched in all the countries of the region at the beginning of the reform process led to an explosive inflationary surge, which had an immediate impact on wages. Quite simply, wage rises lagged well behind, and when they did start to rise at rates comparable to price rises, governments were encouraged to adopt a strict incomes policy. As a result, nominal wages lagged well behind consumer prices, and overall average real wages fell rapidly and substantially in all the countries of the region (figure 2.1). In Poland, they fell by 27% in 1990; in 1991, they fell by more than 42% in Bulgaria, 26% in the Czech Republic and 17% in Romania. They continued to fall in 1992, 1993 and 1994 in Romania, but also in other countries.

Yet it has been in the two largest countries of the region where the decline has been sharpest and most sustained. In Russia, the erosion of real wages was very strong—by more than 40% in 1990, 30% in 1991, and nearly 60% in 1992. In Ukraine, average real wages started to fall rapidly when wage indexation was abolished in early 1992. Although nominal wages in 1994 were 3,078 times higher than in 1990, that rise lagged well behind the rise in the consumer price index. In 1993, real wages fell by nearly 60%, due to inflation of over 10,000%. As a result of this hyperinflation, real wages fell by nearly 70% between 1990 and 1993 (figure 2.1). In that time, average wages also fell below the subsistence minimum. By early 1994, they had fallen to less than 40% of the official poverty line.[2] The erosion of real wages was also very strong in small countries, such as Estonia, where real wages declined by more than 55% between 1990 and 1993.

The desire to contain inflation, coupled with tight budgetary constraints, also imposed downward pressure on the minimum wage. With the exception of Poland (and to a lesser extent Estonia), where the starting level of the minimum wage was extremely low in 1990 (being 19% of the average wage), in all the countries of the region, the minimum wage fell in relation to average earnings (figure 2.2).

This was particularly the case in those countries that suffered from high rates of inflation, such as Romania and Bulgaria. In Romania, over 1991 and 1992, the minimum wage fell from 62% of the average wage to 45%, at a time

---

[2] ILO-CEET: 'Reforming Wage Policy in a Hyperinflationary Context', in *The Ukrainian Challenge: Reforming Labour Market and Social Policy* (CEU Press, 1995).

Figure 2.1 *Changes in Average Real Wages, 1990–94 (%)*

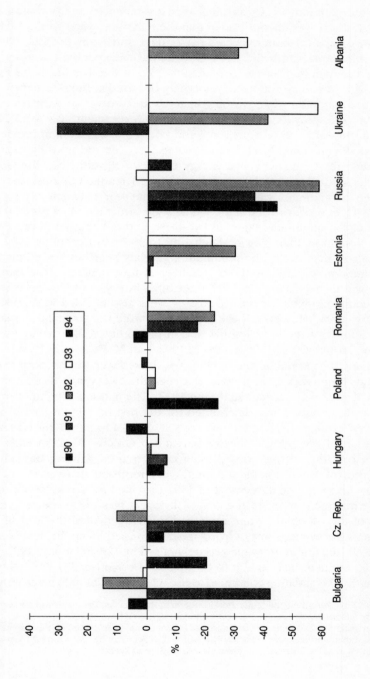

Source: Official figures from the countries concerned, usually from their central statistical offices.

when the minimum wage was acting as an instrument to control wage growth. In 1991, the Government decided that the minimum wage would be raised by 25% compared to an expected rise of 60%, and again, in 1992, 1993 and 1994 minimum wages did not follow actual or expected inflation. As a result, the minimum wage had fallen to 35% of the average wage by July 1994. An even more serious development occurred in Bulgaria, where since 1990 the minimum wage was negotiated and fixed within a tripartite commission of employers, trade unions and the Government. It was calculated on the basis of a 'subsistence level' and prices of a basket of approximately 390 goods, including food, clothes, shoes, services and housing expenses, including rent, electricity and energy charges. Nevertheless, the Government took advantage of the breakdown of the Tripartite Commission in 1991 to keep the minimum wage unchanged for one year, between July 1991 and July 1992, in order to control the whole wage structure. As a result, the real value of the minimum wage fell by 48.3%, and fell relative to the average wage from more than 85% in March 1991 to 30.7% in December 1992.[3]

Similarly in Albania, the minimum wage has been set according to the consumption of basic goods by a family of four persons. The minimum wage was increased once in 1992, three times in 1993 and only once in 1994. Two compensations for price increases were also decided in August 1992 and July 1993. However, these adjustments were not sufficient to maintain the minimum wage in real terms, and in proportion to the average wage it declined from 66% in 1990 to 40% in 1992, and 30.5% in 1993.[4]

In the Czech Republic and in Hungary, the reduction in proportion to the average wage was more modest between the two years, though in both cases, the fall was substantial during 1992. The national minimum wage in the Czech Republic was determined for the first time by a general agreement in February 1991, at the level of CSK 2,000 a month. This was mainly the result of emerging collective bargaining (*Decree No.2*) in early 1991, which introduced the principles of collective bargaining between the Government, trade unions and employers' representatives at the national level.[5] Although the agreement of 1991 provided for a regular adjustment of the minimum wage to the cost of living, it was not respected and the level of the minimum wage remained unchanged until the end of 1991. Whereas the average cost of living index increased by 40.7% between 1990 and 1991, the minimum wage was only raised by 10% in January 1992, when the Government increased it to CSK 2,200 (*Decree No. 53*). In 1992, 1993 and early 1994 inflation continued to rise while the minimum wage remained

---

[3] ILO-CEET: 'Reforming the remuneration system in Bulgaria', in *The Bulgarian Challenge: Reforming Labour Market and Social Policy* (Budapest, ILO CEET, 1993).

[4] I am grateful to D. Metohu of the Ministry of Labour (Wage Department) for this information.

[5] This minimum wage was additionally confirmed in February by *Government Decree No. 99* and started to act as the minimum for the whole wage tariff system.

Figure 2.2 *Minimum Wage Compared to Average Wage in Real Terms, 1989–94 (%)*

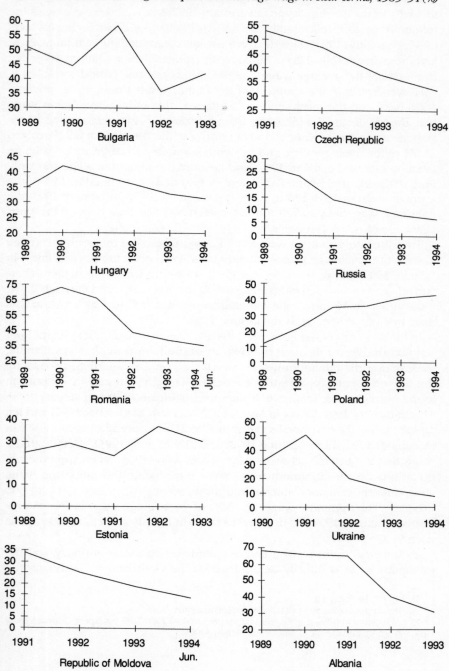

unchanged. As a result, although the minimum wage increased temporarily to 54.2% of the average wage in February 1992, just after the increase of the minimum wage, it fell steadily to 37.3% in 1993 and reached its lowest level of 32.5% in June 1994. This decrease should continue if the minimum wage level remains at CSK 2,200. Similarly in Hungary, the minimum wage fell from 43% of the average wage to 33% during the same period.

However, it is in the countries of the former Soviet Union where the situation has been the most serious. In Russia, although the minimum wage had already declined a long way from its previous close relationship to the average wage, in the early period of reforms in the late 1980s it fell sharply to 23.6% of the average wage and this ratio continued to deteriorate. With an inflation rate of 2,600% in 1992, and because the minimum wage was only irregularly adjusted by the Parliament or President, it declined to 14% of the average wage in 1991 and to 5.6% at the end of 1992. In January 1993, the minimum wage was 20,500 roubles, which was less than 6.5% of the average wage of 320,000 roubles.

The situation was even worse in Ukraine, where the minimum wage fell to 7.8% of the average wage—already itself well below the poverty line—in January 1994, compared to 53% in 1991. This ratio was even smaller in certain relatively privileged industries, such as the fuel (2.9%) and the coal (2.8%) industries.[6] In Moldova, the minimum wage also fell in real terms, to less than 14% of the average wage in June 1994.

In the countries of the Baltic area, the situation was better, though anything but favourable for those at the bottom of the labour market. In Estonia, for instance, the minimum wage was adjusted only on an irregular basis by the Government. As a result, it reached its highest levels in proportion to the average wage immediately after the adjustments (30% in January 1990, 31% in January 1991, 28.6% in March 1992, and 40% in October 1992) and fell rapidly during the few months afterwards (to 21% in December 1990, 18.9% in December 1991, 18.5% in June 1992, and 27% in June 1993).[7] Although the wage fixing mechanisms were reformed in April 1993, when tripartite negotiations on the minimum wage were introduced, the minimum wage subsequently remained unchanged at its level of October 1992, at 300 kroons.[8] The minimum wage was 30% of the average wage before the reforms in January 1990 and declined to 18.5% in June 1992. In June 1993, it had risen to 27%.

In Slovenia, there is no tripartite committee on incomes policy and the minimum wage is directly determined by the Government. Although the

---

[6] ILO-CEET, 1995, op. cit.
[7] See the Appendix for more detailed statistics on trends.
[8] M. Lokk: 'Minimum Wage in Estonia', paper prepared for ILO-CEET Budapest, Estonian Trade Union Research and Development Centre, Tallinn, 1994.

trade unions and the Chamber of Economy (nominally representative of employers) are consulted on this issue, the Government is not obliged to take into account their proposals and, according to the trade unions, only rarely do so.[9] The minimum wage in Slovenia fell in real terms, and fell from 44% of the average wage in July 1991 to 35% in March 1993.

In contrast with other countries, in Poland there was a steady improvement of the minimum wage level in proportion to the average wage.[10] Although the level of the minimum wage was particularly low before the reforms (11.6% in 1989), the reverse trend could be observed after 1989 (19% in 1990, 34.7% in 1991, 37% in 1992 and 41% in 1993; figure 2.2).[11] This was due to three specific features of the minimum wage fixing process in Poland. First, despite the absence of an explicit and direct link with inflation, the minimum wage was regularly adjusted every quarter on the basis of the growth of the costs of living.[12] Second, as stipulated in the Labour Code, the negotiations on minimum wages involved only the Ministry of Labour and the trade unions (*Decree of 14 August 1990*). The absence of the employers gave more negotiation power to the trade unions. Third, the Government—in consultation with the trade unions—decided to disconnect social benefits from the minimum wage, which permitted the latter to be increased more frequently.

The different mechanisms of the minimum wage fixing process were thus reflected in the evolution of the minimum wage level in Central and Eastern Europe between 1990 and 1993. In most countries, step–by–step negotiations did not succeed in maintaining the purchasing power of minimum wages. And in those countries where a tripartite negotiation system was adopted, the change did not prevent the erosion of the minimum wage, and was insufficient to counterbalance the effects of inflation or those of restrictive incomes policies. In this regard, a regular indexing mechanism seems to be more successful, particularly in the immediate aftermath of price liberalisation. However, the role of the trade unions remains potentially important. Even in Poland, despite the existence of an indexing mechanism that was

[9] S. Skledar: 'Minimum Wage in Slovenia', paper prepared for ILO-CEET Budapest, Confederation of New Trade Unions of Slovenia, Ljubljana, August 1993.

[10] Not only was the purchasing power of the minimum wage maintained, but it included new goods in the basket, such as children's and adults' clothing and shoes from August 1992, and expenditure on leisure and adult education from July 1993, so that households living at the minimum wage level could buy more goods and diversify their consumption.

[11] The jump from 19% in 1990 to 34.7% in 1991 was partly due to a change in methodology. While the minimum wage included only basic wage rates until September 1990, it then began to cover all wage elements. However, it continued to increase in proportion to the average wage in 1991 and 1992. See Chapter 4.

[12] The Central Statistical Office calculates the minimum wage by multiplying the average expenditure (mainly on food, heating, rent, education for children, and transport) of a worker belonging to the poorest 20% of the labour force by the coefficient 1.8, which was raised to 1.9 in January 1991.

supposed to be applied each quarter, the Government decided to freeze the minimum wage during the second quarter of 1993 and to postpone its increase in the third quarter, when it was raised from ZL 1,500,000 to 1,650,000.

3. Social Implications

Far more importantly than the changing relationship with the average wage, in every country in the region for which we have data the minimum wage fell to well below the poverty line or the official level of subsistence income (figures 2.3 and 2.4). At the percentage of the average wage to which they had fallen, the minimum wages had lost their function as a minimum level of subsistence for workers and ceased to act as an anchor of the social protection system.

Consider by far the biggest country in the region, with its population of nearly 150 million. In Russia, for some time now the minimum wage has been well below the subsistence wage. While what is known as the 'physiological minimum' was evaluated at 1,759 roubles in April 1992, the minimum wage was only 342 roubles.[13] In September 1992, the physiological minimum was estimated to be 2,963 roubles while the minimum wage had been changed to 900 roubles. Surprisingly, the Government decided to change the methods of calculation of the physiological minimum in November 1992, and drastically lowered the minimum quantities of consumption (such as reducing the minimum level of meat from 54 kilograms for one person per year to 27.5 kilograms). The differences between the two methods made a substantial difference to income needs. According to the new basket of goods, the physiological minimum in January 1993 was 5,353 roubles but would have been 8,534 roubles with the previous methodology. Nevertheless, the minimum wage, which was still 900 roubles in January 1993, fell to 16.8% of the physiological minimum.[14] In January 1995, the minimum wage was 12.3% of the physiological minimum.

In Ukraine, as in Russia and other parts of the Commonwealth of Independent States, the minimum wage has been used as an instrument to control the whole tariff system. In early 1992, when the minimum wage had nearly reached the subsistence level (94%), the Government decided to abolish the wage indexation system, so that the minimum wage started again to fall

---

[13] The 'physiological minimum' is calculated by the Ministry of Labour and includes a basket of essential goods, mainly food. According to the trade unions, this minimum would not be sufficient for survival and they have proposed a 'normative minimum', which includes a larger number of goods. To give an example, the physiological minimum as calculated by the Government was 5,535 roubles in January 1993, while the normative minimum as calculated by the trade unions was more than 15,000 roubles. The minimum wage was a mere 900 roubles.

[14] Chetvernina, ibid.

well below the poverty line. By early 1994, the minimum wage had fallen to an incredible 4% of the subsistence minimum, although wage regulations still stipulated that the minimum wage should not be fixed below the poverty line.

Similarly in Estonia, whereas the minimum wage remained unchanged at the level of 300 kroons in 1992 and 1993 (corresponding to a net wage of 292 kroons after income tax), by July 1993 the physiological minimum was estimated at 490 kroons. As in Russia, this physiological minimum is a critical minimum that includes only basic expenditure. The social minimum, which includes more goods, was estimated at 700 kroons. According to Estonian trade unions, it is impossible to survive with the minimum wage and workers were able to do so only because of the state subsidy for rent and family support and because many of them worked on a piece of land. However, a growing proportion of Estonian workers were unable to pay their rent in 1993 and 1994 and the incidence of poverty has been worsening.[15]

In some countries the situation did improve. In Romania, although the minimum wage remained for a long time well below 50% of the subsistence minimum, when the Government in July 1993 increased the minimum wage from 17,600 to 30,000 lei, it reached 79% of the poverty line. Similarly in Bulgaria, the minimum wage in March 1994 represented 70% of the subsistence minimum, compared to 32% just one year before.

Those were exceptions, however. In Albania, the Ministry of Finance and Economy uses 17 items for calculating the minimum subsistence level, which was 2,934 leks in 1992. At the same time, the minimum wage was 675 leks, well below the subsistence minimum. The absence of an official subsistence minimum in Albania makes it difficult to compare it to the minimum wage, which was, however, below 50% of the subsistence minimum in May 1995, according to trade union estimates (figure 2.3).

In Hungary, the minimum level for the standard of living was estimated by the Central Statistical Office in early 1993 as HUF 14,000 a month for one individual (not for a family) while the minimum wage in early 1993 was HUF 8,000 (increased to HUF 9,000 in February 1993, to HUF 10,500 in February 1994, and to HUF 12,200 in February 1995). According to a survey carried out by the Hungarian trade union MSZOSZ, as a direct result of price liberalisation, in 1991 and 1992 over half of the families had reduced their consumption of meat and cheese, and no longer bought any of the better quality foodstuffs. A large proportion of families also indicated that their consumption of certain foods could not be reduced any further.[16]

In Poland, although its purchasing power increased from 1991, the minimum wage still does not satisfy indispensable needs and represented

---

[15] According to the Estonian Trade Union Research and Development Centre, 1994; Lokk, 1994, op. cit.
[16] I. Ékes: 'The experience of the sample survey done on the consumption structure of the Hungarian population', Economic and Social Research Institute, MSZOSZ, Budapest, 1993.

Figure 2.3 *Minimum Wage and Subsistence Minimum (official) Levels*

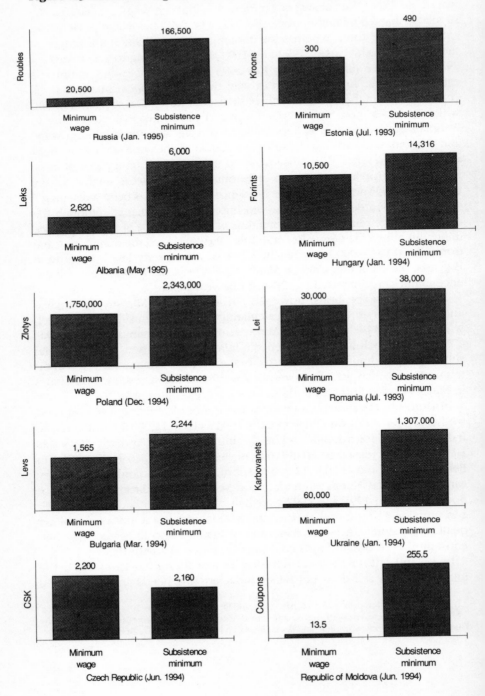

only 74.6% of the subsistence minimum in December 1993.[17] From 75% of the subsistence minimum in 1981, it fell to 47% in 1990 and then increased in 1991 (68%), 1992 (75%) and 1993 (78%).

Only in the Czech Republic was the minimum wage fixed above an official measure of poverty, after its adjustment to CSK 2,200 in January 1992. However, the minimum wage was not changed for almost two years after that, while inflation raised the income needed to meet subsistence needs. However, the minimum wage tariff was increased in December 1993, from CSK 2,200 to 2,340.

To appreciate the full extent of the deterioration, one must recognise that the falls in the minimum wage in most countries occurred at a time of severe cuts in free or subsidised services, such as education, housing and health, which characterised the old collectivist system, thus making life even more difficult for people in the poorest categories.[18]

In order to protect the purchasing power of the incomes of those in the most vulnerable groups, the government in some countries decided to retain price controls over some basic goods. In Romania, the Government did not liberalise the prices of bread, milk, sugar, meat, public transport and state housing rents before April 1992, a policy that was also partially followed in Bulgaria. However, this was the source of an increasing gap between the minimum wage and the general price level of other goods. In some countries, the list of goods covered has been incomplete, excluding the cost of housing, other basic commodities and services, so that the minimum wage became rapidly disconnected from reality.

The fact that the minimum wage was well below the subsistence minimum induced most employers to pay wages above the official minimum wage. According to official statistics, in most countries the percentage of workers paid at the minimum wage level has been low compared to Western European countries.[19]

This has been most strikingly the case in countries where the fall of the minimum wage has been the greatest. In Ukraine, for instance, in April 1993, when the minimum wage was 4,600 karbovanets, 1.5% of full–time workers received less than that level, 0.9% received between 4,600 and 5,000 karbovanets, and 6.9% had a wage between 5,000 and 8,000 karbovanets. In Bulgaria, the share of full–time workers receiving the minimum wage in industry was 3.5% in 1991. In Russia, according to official statistics, the

---

[17] According to the trade union Solidarnosc, 1993; E. Tomaszewska and E. Urbanowicz: 'Minimum Wage in Poland', Report prepared for ILO-CEET Budapest, Lodz, 1993.
[18] G. Standing: 'Restructuring for Distributive Justice in Eastern Europe', ILO-CEET Policy Paper No.2, Budapest, January 1993.
[19] S. Bazen and G. Benhayoun (eds.): *Low Pay and Minimum Wages*, International Journal of Manpower Human Resources, Vol 15, Nos. 2/3, 1994.

real incomes of all groups of the active population are substantially higher than the fixed minimum and approached the average wage.[20] At the end of 1994, 0.9% of the working population were paid the minimum wage. In the Czech Republic, in 1992 only 0.3% were earning less than the minimum wage and less than 2% were earning the minimum wage.[21] In Poland, less than 4% were at the minimum wage level in 1989. Although it increased to 6.7% in 1992, less than 10% of the working population would be paid today at the minimum wage level.

This percentage is higher in Estonia, where about 10% of full–time employees receive less than the minimum wage.[22] In Albania, a survey carried out among 140 enterprises showed that around 16% of workers received the minimum wage in 1991.[23] According to a recent ILO survey among all industrial enterprises, in September 1994, less than 5% of workers were paid the official minimum wage.[24] The different chapters in this book present a similar picture in other countries of the region.

Critics of the minimum wage as a mechanism for protecting low–paid workers would see these small proportions of the labour force at the minimum wage level as a sign of the inefficiency of the minimum wage, not only as an instrument of social protection but also as an economic tool to influence the whole wage structure, and the need for dismantling the minimum wage mechanism, leaving wage determination to market forces.

This reasoning would be dubious. There are at least five characteristics of the emerging labour market that need to be borne in mind.

First, there are reasons for thinking that the numbers of workers paid only the minimum wage are underestimated, since there is considerable anecdotal evidence that many employers pay wages lower than the minimum wage level despite the law. This hidden phenomenon is difficult to estimate but would seem to be widespread in some countries, such as Russia and Ukraine, where effective instruments and procedures for labour market regulation have yet to be developed or implemented. In the non–budgetary sphere in Russia, some employers close to bankruptcy were able legally to violate minimum wage regulations by postponing the payment of minimum wages after the statutory term.

Second, although paid more than the minimum wage level, in some countries a majority of workers are still paid below the subsistence level. This has been the case in Russia, where 10% of the population lived far

[20] See Chapter 3.
[21] See Chapter 6.
[22] Lokk, 1994, op. cit.
[23] D. Metohu: 'Minimum wage in Albania', report prepared for ILO-CEET Budapest, Tirana, August 1993.
[24] See by the same author: 'Restructuring Wages Under Crisis Conditions: Results of the Enterprise Survey in Albanian Industry', ILO-CEET Report, Budapest, June 1995.

below the poverty line in 1993, with a per capita income of less than twice the minimum wage. Another 27% of the population had incomes ranging from two to four minimum wages, which was still under the physiological minimum. This means that nearly 40% of the population have an income below the subsistence minimum.[25]

Third, national statistics conceal considerable differences between industries and between regions. There is a large proportion of workers at the minimum wage level in some sectors or regions which have been particularly affected by the current reforms. For instance, in the trade sector in the Czech Republic, 37.3% of workers were paid below the minimum wage, compared to a national average of 0.3%. The largest proportion of low–paid workers are in the food industry, but also in engineering, the electro–technical industry, wood, paper and textile industries, agriculture, transport and printing. These branches are generally characterised by low productivity and a low–skilled labour force and have generally a high share of female workers (as in textile or food industries) and part–time employees (construction, trade and service). According to national data analysed by Buchtikova in Chapter 6, female workers represent more than 60% of low–paid workers and the likelihood of getting lower wages is much higher among young workers between 16 and 19 and part–time workers. The groups with the lowest income in Poland are those employed in the sphere of non–material production such as in education, health, culture and art but also in agriculture. Women are also the most seriously hit by the decline in real wages.[26] High proportions of workers received below the minimum wage level in Estonia, Hungary, Bulgaria, but also in other countries these levels are paid in the agriculture sector. In Bulgaria, the highest share of workers paid the minimum wage were in trade (4.2%), clothing (14%) and pulp and paper (5.6%), but also in heavy industries. Three of the nine districts were most affected by real wage and real minimum wage decline: Michailovgrad, Lovesh and Razgrad, reflecting the predominance of heavy industries. In Russia, as noted in Chapter 3, low incomes were particularly prevalent in the North Caucasus, where in 1992 the income of the richest 10% reached 22 times the income of the poorest 10%.[27]

Fourth, the decline in the minimum wage influences not only workers at the bottom of the wage and grading scale but also most categories of workers, whose wage is determined on the basis of the minimum wage. Particularly in the state sector, and most of all in the so–called 'budgetary' sector (public services), the wages of all groups are based on some multiple

---

[25] According to the State Statistics Committee of Russia.
[26] According to the trade union Solidarnosc, Tomaszewska and Urbanowicz, 1993, op. cit.
[27] Chapter 3.

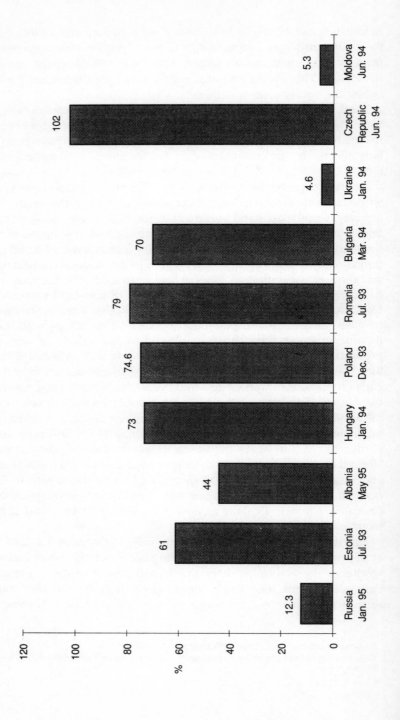

Figure 2.4 *Ratio of Minimum Wage to Subsistence Minimum Level (%)*

of the minimum wage. Their real wages fell dramatically in most countries, leading to important economic problems that we identify in section 6.

Finally, because social benefits have been linked to the minimum wage, the decline of the latter also led to an erosion in the value of unemployment benefits, child care allowances and in some countries other social benefits. Maintaining a constant nominal minimum wage during prolonged periods from 1991 to 1994 was a means by which policy makers at the time controlled public expenditure, since many public payments were tied to the minimum wage, including not only the pay of employees in the budget sphere, but also unemployment benefits, school and university grants, retirement pensions and child allowances. All fell in real terms.

In Hungary, pensions followed the decline in the minimum wage, declining from 29% of the average wage in 1991 to 23% in 1993. Average unemployment benefits reached 36% of the average wage compared to 41% during the same period. This erosion of social protection contributed to worsen the social situation and contradicts the claim made recently for cutting social expenditures in Hungary.[28] According to recent surveys, the number of people living under the subsistence minimum would have increased from one to three million since 1990.[29] In Russia, social benefits calculated on the basis of the minimum wage also experienced a dramatic decline. In some cases, the low minimum wage led to a perverted system, in which unemployment benefits and minimum pensions were above the minimum wage level.[30] However, the former were not too high, since they were also well below any reasonable notion of subsistence.

While the fall in minimum wages in real terms implied an erosion of social benefits, the fact that social benefits were linked to the minimum wage discouraged governments from increasing the minimum wage. In Estonia, for instance, the minimum wage remained unchanged for a long time because it was linked to the social security system, which faced a budgetary crisis.[31]

In Poland, faced by the same constraints for increasing the minimum wage, the trade unions and the Government decided in December 1991 to link unemployment benefits to the average wage instead of the minimum wage. This change of calculation method made it possible to raise the minimum wage a few weeks later, in January 1992. A similar reform is needed in other countries, because this would allow increases in the minimum wage while freeing it from excessive pressure. In the past, we saw the incomes of the

[28] R. Rose in the *AMEX Bank Review*, Budapest, November 1992.
[29] Ékes, 1993, op. cit.
[30] For detailed figures, see Chapter 3.
[31] Out of a population of 1.5 million, 450,000 Estonians are dependent on the social security system. Pensions are fixed at 85% and unemployment benefits at 60% of the minimum wage; Lokk, 1994, op. cit.

poorest people, which were linked only to a few basic items (whose prices are normally kept under control), becoming gradually isolated from general price increases, thus worsening conditions of social exclusion. Moreover, it corresponds in some cases to a wish by some governments to reduce social benefits so as to channel more resources into economic reforms. In fact, one wonders whether the only role of the minimum wage in the transition period was not precisely to help governments to reduce social protection.

4. Problems of Efficiency and Productivity

Apart from leading to social unrest, this trend also had important economic implications. The most serious relates to productivity and efficiency. According to the efficiency wage theory, downward pressure on wages could have the effect of lowering worker motivation and increasing absenteeism. Wages above the average would increase incentives to work and lead to productivity improvements, through lower absenteeism and labour turnover, better maintenance of equipment and better adaptation to new technologies.

While several efficiency wage behaviours have been identified in Western enterprises through empirical studies,[32] the *'nutritional'* version of the efficiency theory seems to be particularly adapted to the current situation in Central and Eastern Europe.[33] This approach focuses on the connection between higher wages and workers' health. It assumes that workers' productivity can be increased by better nutrition and that the cost to the employer of higher payment is outweighed by their increased output. This implies that workers should receive a minimum subsistence wage to allow them to meet their nutritional needs and thus be more productive.

In fact, how could workers work efficiently if their income is lower than the subsistence minimum? In Romania, there has been a worsening pattern of poverty and malnutrition, which have been the most worrying features of the Romanian 'transition', with adverse effects on production.[34] Also, growing

---

[32] For a survey, see L. A. Riveros and L. Bouton: 'Efficiency wage theory, labour markets, and adjustment', Working Paper Series 731, Washington DC, World Bank, July 1991. The minimum wage as an efficiency wage payment has also been noticed in some developing countries. For instance, shortly after independence, some East African countries used minimum wages to raise the average level of wages in an effort to break migratory employment and to establish a 'high wage' economy; G. Starr: *Minimum Wage Fixing* (Geneva, International Labour Office, 1981).

[33] Riveros and Bouton, 1991, op. cit.; G. B. Rodgers: 'Nutritionally based wage determination in the low–income labour market', *Oxford Economic Papers*, New Series No.1, Mar. 1975, pp. 61–81; J. E. Stiglitz: 'Wage determination and unemployment in LDC's', in *Quarterly Journal of Economics*, May 1974, pp. 194–227.

[34] C. Zamfir: 'The Romanian wage system in the transition to a market economy', World Employment Programme Working Paper No. 54, Geneva, ILO, January 1992.

absenteeism, a phenomenon observed in most enterprises in Central and Eastern Europe, is directly related to time spent on a second job aimed at increasing total income.

The fact that most enterprises pay more than the minimum wage even for the lowest skilled provides evidence of an efficiency wage process: although some enterprises could pay less, they pay more to maintain normal production.[35] It shows that minimum wages are not fixed at a level at which workers would increase their motivation and productivity. In Estonia, the sharp decrease in real wage had important adverse effects on productivity.[36] Many strikes interrupted production in Bulgaria, Romania, and elsewhere. Strikes mainly disrupted the sectors most affected by the restrictive income policy, such as the budget sector, among doctors, nurses, teachers, transport workers and public employees, as well as in the metal industry.[37]

A tax–based incomes policy also has direct effects on the quality of the labour force. In Hungary in 1991, almost 50% of the families interrupted their expenditures on cultural entertainment, and there was no expenditure on culture in 55% of households.[38] How will people who are not able to spend on newspapers, theatre, holidays, etc., be able to develop new skills and to keep pace with technological progress? How, if their whole budget is spent on basic goods, will they be able to continue to finance the education of their children?

All these effects contribute to a deterioration in human capital and might lead to an increase in the number of unskilled workers. They underline the perverse effects of the policy often proposed, that the minimum for living should not include goods other than those strictly necessary for basic subsistence.[39] Not only may this policy have adverse social effects, it may also be economically misleading, at the moment when economists, employers and policymakers put emphasis on the virtues of a strong educational system and on the need to increase skills in order to face new technological challenges.

---

[35] In Bulgaria, for instance, the wage fund ceiling system did not deter enterprises from increasing wages. Many enterprises decided to increase wages above the ceiling and pay the corresponding tax in order to increase workers' motivation and productivity. This process was mainly observed in the most profitable sectors, such as chemicals and the electrical and electronics industry. ILO-CEET, 1993, op. cit.

[36] J. Sillaste and U. Purga: 'Level of living, wages, and labour market in Estonia', Estonian Trade Unions Research and Development Centre, Tallinn, June 1993.

[37] This led in Romania and Bulgaria to a process of approaching claims separately, as they occurred. This counterproductive policy led to an avalanche of wage claims, which threatened political authority and the stability of the reform programme. For Bulgaria, see ILO-CEET, 1993, op. cit., pp. 52–53: for Romania, see Zamfir, 1992, op. cit.

[38] Ékes, 1993, op. cit.

[39] World Bank: *Poland: Income Support and the Social Safety Net: Policies for the Transition* (Washington DC, World Bank, June 1992).

5. Minimum Wage and Employment

Traditionally it has been argued that minimum wages would have a negative impact on employment. Although there is no convincing empirical work in this area,[40] this argument has often been presented in Central and Eastern Europe. In the current period, it is difficult to test such an argument, for three main reasons. First, most enterprises are launching important restructuring programmes including layoffs without any consideration of the level of minimum wage. Second, the level of the minimum wage is so low in these countries that it could not have a negative effect on employment. Third, it covers such a small portion of employees that it should not induce enterprises to reduce employment. The question, however, should probably be asked in the following way: if the Government raises the minimum wage in proportion to the average wage, and introduces indexation mechanisms, could this affect the employment of the lowest categories of workers? This might be the case, not in the economy as a whole but in some sectors or enterprises particularly hard hit by the fall of production and where higher levels of the minimum wage could not be paid. At the same time, one might question the impact of excessively low minimum wages on the restructuring process: would firms not be inclined to maintain employment and low wages and avoid or postpone restructuring?

One study on the Czech Republic (presented in Chapter 6 by A. Buchtikova) tried to measure what the impact of increasing minimum wages would be on employment, through a two–stage process: first, by testing the respective impacts of different levels of minimum wages above the official rate on enterprises' total wage bill, and second, by analysing the effects of these new wage bill levels on employment. The main result was that the effect of the growth of the minimum wage on employment would be marginal. In fact, the increase of the minimum wage to different levels above the current minimum, even by twice its official amount (CSK 24 instead of the current 12 per hour) would not induce employers to cut the number of employees by more than 1% above that expected in the restructuring process. This confirms that the minimum wage level in the current process could be raised without having a substantial adverse effect on employment. This phenomenon probably holds for other countries, since most enterprises pay well above the official minimum.

The study on the Czech Republic also shows that adjustment of the minimum wage could have greater effects in some sectors. These are generally

---

[40] For a survey of empirical studies, see S. Bazen and G. Benhayoun in Chapter 10; see also R. Freeman: 'Labour market institutions and policies: Help or hindrance to economic development?', paper presented at the World Bank Conference on Development Economics, Washington DC, 30 April and 1 May 1992.

industries with a higher percentage of workers at the minimum wage level, and where the percentage of labour costs to total costs is comparatively high. They are also characterised by financial problems and low productivity. Industries such as food and wood and the electrical and engineering industries would not be able to absorb the growth of the minimum wage without a reduction of their workforce. Moreover, most vulnerable groups would be particularly hard hit by this process.

This leads to two conclusions. First, there are weak grounds for believing minimum wage increases will have adverse effects on employment. Of course, we need more empirical studies on this matter but it appears that the negative role of the minimum wage in respect of employment has been over-emphasised in order to support a policy aimed at using the minimum wage to control wage growth. Second, this study indicates that the minimum wage could be raised only progressively in some industries, and points to the need to consider the problems of the minimum wage by individual industries rather than only from a national perspective.

In contrast, other studies have shown that low wages have induced employers to delay the restructuring of their firms. In Romania, there are reports that some enterprises have decided upon moderate wage rises in order to avoid having to dismiss a large number of workers.[41] In Bulgaria, to the extent that it operated, the wage fund ceiling as part of the incomes policy tended to limit layoffs, creating an obstacle to restructuring.[42]

6. Labour Force Fragmentation

Since 1990, there has been increasing labour force fragmentation between those in budget organisations, whose wage has been relatively strongly linked to the minimum wage, and those in other sectors.

In most of the countries, the minimum wage is still used for calculating salaries in the budgetary sphere. In Russia, for instance, starting wages of the grading schedule in budget organisations correspond to the minimum wage. Fixed at a same amount for many years, they tended to be slightly above the national minimum wage in 1992 and 1993.[43] The amount paid to other grades of employee is determined by multiplying the minimum rate by the ratio provided for their respective category. For example, in January 1993, when the minimum wage was 1,800 roubles, a teacher or a doctor according to the 10th category received 7,182 roubles (1,800 x 3.99).[44] Because of this link to the minimum wage, employees of the budgetary sphere

---

[41] Zamfir, 1992, op. cit., p. 14.
[42] ILO-CEET, 1993, op. cit.
[43] For instance fixed at 4,500 roubles against 4,275 for the national minimum wage in April 1993.
[44] See Chapter 3.

have proved to be in a disadvantaged position. As of March 1992, the average wage in the budgetary sphere was lower than the average wage by approximately 50%. By March 1993, the national average was 22,000 roubles whereas the maximum possible salary in the budgetary sphere, for the eighteenth category at the top of the wage grading scale, was 22,657 roubles. This situation would automatically change if the minimum wage was increased and would gradually approach the subsistence minimum. Similar problems are emerging in Poland, where the Government has also restrained wages in the budgetary sphere through the crude instrument of the minimum wage. The most affected employees have been in health, education, science and culture. As a result, between 1990 and 1993 the average wage in the budgetary sector dropped by 30% in comparison with the national average. Bearing in mind that the national average wage was declining in real terms by more than 30%, we can appreciate how substantial was the purchasing power lost by budget employees in the period. In 1992 many teachers and other employees in public education received salaries that were below the minimum wage level, which led to trade union action.[45] The resultant improvements scarcely last long. In 1993, the poor financial situation in the budget sector was cited as the main factor justifying the Government's decision to freeze the national minimum wage, and again teachers and others suffered disproportionately.

7. Disconnection from the Wage Scale

While they influenced wages in the budget sector, the minimum wages started to be disconnected from the whole wage and grading scale. Because they are fixed at very low and constant levels, minimum wages do not influence wage grading as a whole anymore. In Russia, for instance, the different adjustments of the minimum wage did not exert any influence on the growth of the average wage. From April to December 1992, the average monthly wage rose from 3,052 to 16,071 roubles while the minimum wage remained at 900 roubles. On the other hand, a minimum wage increase to 2,250 roubles in February 1992 was not reflected in the growth of the average wage (wages being mainly determined according to the subsidies given to different sectors or regions, as discussed in chapter 3).[46]

Since Poland is the only country where the minimum wage increased in proportion to the average wage during the economic reforms, it is interesting to analyse the role that the minimum wage played within the whole wage scale. As shown in table 2.1, the minimum wage in 1989 had no influence

---

[45] Tomaszewska and Urbanowicz, 1993, op. cit.
[46] This process was also observed in Bulgaria. ILO-CEET, 1993, op. cit.

Table 2.1 *Minimum Wage, Lowest Wages and Average Wages, Poland, 1989–92*

	1989	1990	1991	1992
Minimum wage	23 925	220 667	613 750	1 087 500
Average wage	206 758	1 050 900	1 756 300	2 983 200
Average earnings of employees in the first grade	96 872	–	657 000	1 228 000
% of remuneration in the first grade compared to the average wage	46.9	–	37.4	41.2
% of the earnings of employees of the first grade compared to the minimum wage	404.8	–	107.0	112.9

Source: Solidarnosc, 1993.

on the wage structure since wages of the first grade, that is, of the first group of workers, at the bottom, were four times the minimum wage. Since 1991, when the minimum wage started to be adjusted to inflation, it has been regarded as the basis for the whole wage structure: wages of the first group were determined according to the minimum wage, and were fixed just slightly above that level, by 7%. This did not imply a decrease in the wages of this first category with regard to the average wage (41.2% of the average wage in 1992 against 37.4% in 1991). This means that a closer linkage between the minimum wage and wages at different grades, especially those at the bottom, does not systematically lead, as is sometimes argued, to downward pressure on wages, especially of the lowest paid categories.

Some specialists have argued that using the minimum wage as the basis of the whole wage system might lead to a compression of the wage scale and lower wage differentials. This is a complex issue, to which easy answers do not exist. On the one hand, the payment of the minimum wage should not prevent employers from continuing or implementing a payment system that rewards skills and performance for a category or for all employees. Minimum wage and wage differentials were simultaneously increased in Poland in 1991 and 1992. Some examples in Bulgaria also show that it was possible to increase the minimum wage in 1993 while continuing to increase wage differentials to reward high skills and good individual or collective performance in some profitable enterprises. On the other hand, the difficult economic conditions faced by most enterprises in Central and Eastern Europe show that the minimum wage should not be increased without taking into account the ability of enterprises to pay. While the minimum wage could play a regulatory role within the wage grading system, high increases in the minimum wages without consideration of economic and financial potential might worsen economic and social problems in some enterprises and sectors and have a perverse effect. They could induce employers to cut previous payment systems based on skills and productivity in order to respect the minimum wage level as fixed by the law. This might influence investment decisions and lead to a change in the skills and qualifications of labour employed. There is clearly a balance to be found here. We will argue later that a decentralised approach might help in differentiating the minimum wage policy according to the economic and social context.

8. Disruption of the Income Structure

The erosion of real average wages and minimum wages has implied a recomposition of the income structure, with a trend towards nonmonetary sources of income. In Bulgaria, for instance, the restrictive incomes policy led to the occurrence of four phenomena.[47]

First, the wage proportion of total income decreased from 44.8% of total income in 1990 to 35.3% in 1992, with a trend towards the substitution of wage income by income from 'other economic activities'.[48] The latter increased from 4.6% of the total in 1991 to 19.9% in 1992.[49] This high percentage included income from second, non–regular private jobs, since the sharp fall of real wages in 1991 induced workers to complement their main activities with additional jobs. The growth of this source was spectacular in the years of 1991 and 1992, which were also marked by a growth of temporary and precarious jobs, unable to offer a sufficient income.

Second, social payments fell from 18.4% of total income in 1991 to 16.5% in 1992. The decline was mainly due to the collapse of the Tripartite Commission and the irregularity of minimum wage adjustments. The absence of minimum wage growth reflected on social security payments, which suffered the strongest decline of all income sources in 1992.[50]

Third, the nonmonetary share of income increased in 1990 and 1991. This was mainly due to the high consumption by households of their own

---

[47] For a more detailed description, see ILO-CEET, 1993, op. cit., pp. 50–51.

[48] M. Nenova–Amar: 'The labour market in Bulgaria: Wages and employment', paper presented at the World Bank Workshop on the Labour Market in Transitional Socialist Economies, Stirin Castle, Czech Republic, 16–17 April 1993.

[49] Other main sources of monetary income in 1992 were social payments (for 16.5% of total income), and interest from savings (13.7%).

[50] Agency for Economic Co–ordination and Development: 'IV Quarter 1992' and '1992 Report on the state of the Bulgarian Economy', in *Business Survey Series* (Sofia, AECD, 1993).

production, particularly within rural families. From 1990 to 1991, the share of nonmonetary income in agriculture increased from 21.3% to 37.3%.

Fourth, relaxation of the incomes policy in 1992 caused a reverse trend, with a growth of wages relative to nonmonetary forms.

Similar phenomena are observed in other countries. In Russia, in only one year, between 1993 and 1994, the wage share in total monetary income fell from 61% to 47%,[51] and the wage share in total income had fallen well below 40%, with nonmonetary sources of income, mainly farm products, representing more than 20% of total income. The sharp fall in real wages in Estonia in 1992 also had the direct effect of decreasing wages in total income, and of increasing non–monetary sources of income.[52] The need to complement a minimum wage well below the vital physiological minimum pushed many workers to cultivate a small piece of land and to consume their own products.[53] Similarly in Hungary, farm products represented an increasing source of income compared to the basic wage, self–sufficiency representing one way to protect the family against price increases. A significant proportion of families surveyed in 1991 and 1992 produced their own fruit, vegetables, and meat, did their own repair and maintenance jobs, and made their own clothing. Forty five per cent of families tried to increase their income by extra work.[54] This need to earn additional money and to find second jobs pushes a growing proportion of the labour force towards the informal economy. The fact that wages represented a decreasing percentage of total income, and that other sources of income were emerging led some observers to question the need for wages to follow inflation and a need to increase the minimum wage.[55] Yet the emergence of these sources of income was a consequence of restructuring and the incomes policy. Although the appearance of new forms of income reflects many factors, such as the problems of the social protection system and the difficult economic conditions of employers, it is also the sign of the inappropriateness of the tax–based incomes policy, which limited the growth of wages. The growth of non–monetary forms in agriculture to compensate for the fall of regular earnings is significant. Moreover, according to I. Ékes, in Hungary the majority of workers most seriously hit by

---

[51] 'Developments in the Social and Labour Sphere in Russia: Trends, Problems and Ways of Solving Them,' paper presented by the Ministry of Labour during a joint workshop organised with ILO-CEET in Bor, Russia, 1–2 February 1995, mimeo, ILO-CEET, Budapest.

[52] The relationship between inflation and the basic wage in the current transitional phase in Central and Eastern Europe is a complex one, with two opposite trends: while partial indexation normally raises the basic wage in proportion to other benefits, declining real wages induce the development of other sources of monetary and nonmonetary sources of income.

[53] Lokk, 1994, op. cit.

[54] Ékes, 1993, op. cit.

[55] This argument has been made by Nenova–Amar, 1993, op.cit., and by the World Bank in *Bulgaria: An Economic Update* (Washington DC, World Bank Report, May 1993).

the real wage decline have not been able to find another source of income, and because of growing unemployment only a minority of workers were able to acquire two jobs.

In this context, the evolution of real wages, the indexation of minimum wages, and a return to more regular work contracts would help to reduce the diversification of income sources. Conversely, the erosion of real wages, the fall in the value of minimum wages and the growth of precarious jobs would increase labour force fragmentation and social tension.

9. Adverse Effects on Consumption and Savings

Something that has not been stressed in debates on wage developments in the region is the impact of the fall of real average wages and minimum wages on the national level of *consumption*. After the collapse of external markets—in particular in the former USSR—and the crises of domestic markets, enterprises had problems selling their products and a fall of production occurred everywhere, leading to growing unemployment.[56] In this context, the basic 'Keynesian' principle seems to be particularly relevant to Central and Eastern Europe. Raising wages would boost domestic demand, production and employment. If there is a deficiency in aggregate demand, higher wages may stimulate consumption expenditure and thus employment and growth. In Central and Eastern Europe, this could well be the case if those receiving higher incomes do not channel their savings into productive national investment or have consumption patterns biased towards imported and capital–intensive goods. In these circumstances, a shift in the distribution of income towards low–income groups could result in a more labour–intensive pattern of aggregate demand, and hence more jobs.

Many specialists have stressed the need for enterprises in Central and Eastern Europe to find new markets abroad. However, this search for new markets seems to be difficult—as is the case with the countries of the European Union—and should therefore be complemented by the development of a strong domestic market. Moreover, theories of foreign investment have highlighted the need for a strong domestic market to attract foreign companies.[57] Not only does the restriction of domestic consumption limit foreign investment, but a policy based on low wages encourages foreign capital towards the most traditional activities, whose comparative advantage is mainly based on lower labour costs.

---

[56] Commission of the European Communities: 'Employment in Europe: Central and Eastern Europe', Report No.5, Employment Observatory, DGV, Brussels, December 1993.

[57] J. Dunning and G. Norman: 'The location choice of offices of international companies', in *Environment and Planning*, Vol. 19, 1987, pp. 613–631.

There can be no doubt that the early phases of reform have had severe adverse effects on aggregate demand. As noted in Chapter 7 personal consumption in Bulgaria, over a period of four years between 1990 and 1993, fell by 40%, and was expected to continue to fall in 1994 and 1995. In Hungary, according to a survey carried out in 1991–92 on 6,000 households by the Research Institute of the Hungarian trade union MSZOSZ, the effects of price liberalisation on living standards had been substantial. While 50% of the families had to interrupt their expenditure on cultural entertainment, 14 to 27% of the families reduced their expenditure on newspapers, clothing and luxury articles. In 1991, there was no expenditure on culture in 55% of households, on clothing in 17%. Because of the inflation on basic food products, 90% had to increase their budget for expenditure on food and energy.[58]

This situation also led to growing consumption on the black market: unbilled services, non–declared activities or rents, second–hand shopping, shopping at cheap street dealers, hiring illegal ('black') labour to carry out repairs, etc. A survey carried out among 2,000 households showed that a majority of them had increased their consumption on the black market, and that they had spent even greater amounts in this way.[59] This phenomenon generated more than HUF 100 billion of invisible income, and represented 24% of GDP.[60] This process has contributed to limit production in the mainstream, taxable sector.

Changes in wages also have direct effects on savings and investment. In Bulgaria, in combination with an increase in interest rates, the increase in real wages in 1992 after the sharp fall of 1991 boosted domestic savings. As a percentage of income, savings reached 31.8% in the fourth quarter of 1992, compared to 6% in the third quarter of 1991. By contrast, savings fell in 1991 when real wages dropped. Similarly in Hungary, because of the fall in disposable income, about 40% of families that still had savings in 1990 had to use them to preserve their standard of living and for daily expenditure in 1991 and 1992. More than 60% of families were unable to put aside any savings. It is also significant that 90% of households did not engage in any kind of entrepreneurial activity in 1991, more than 40% of them attributing this to a lack of capital.[61]

In this context of falling production, a policy aimed at maintaining real wages and ensuring an acceptable minimum wage could have positive effects on consumption and savings, thus enhancing investment and production.

[58] Ékes, 1993, op. cit.
[59] I. Ékes, *Rejtett gazdaság–láthatatlan jövedelem, tegnap és ma* [Hidden economy—Invisible incomes, yesterday and tomorrow], Budapest, 1993. Henceforth, Ékes, 1993b.
[60] Probably these figures are underestimated, because of the reluctance of consumers to describe their propensity for the informal economy. Other surveys suggest a figure of HUF 500 billion.
[61] Ékes, 1993b, op. cit.

10. Reforming Minimum Wage Policy

Confronted by growing social problems and conflict, most governments in 1993 and 1994 decided to modify their policy with regard to the minimum wage. In Russia, a *Presidential Decree on 'Urgent measures to stabilise the standard of living of the population'* was adopted in March 1993, and the minimum wage was raised several times in 1993 to 4,275 roubles (from 2,250) in April, and then to 7,740 in August, and 14,620 in December. The minimum wage was also increased to 20,500 roubles in July 1994. The latest increase was to 44,700 roubles in April 1995. It was decided to raise progressively the minimum wage towards the officially recognised subsistence minimum. In Estonia, tripartite negotiations in August 1993 concentrated on an increase in the minimum wage. In Hungary, the minimum wage was increased from HUF 8,000 to 9,000 in February 1993, to HUF 10,500 in February 1994, and to 12,200 in February 1995. In Bulgaria, in March 1993, a new incomes policy was introduced to protect incomes from inflation and to readjust the wages of groups most seriously hurt by the first two years of reform. Consequently, the minimum wage, the average gross salary of civil servants and the average pension were compensated for the reduction in real value incurred after July 1992.

(i) Introducing indexation mechanisms

In its reforms of 1993 the Bulgarian Government also created a system of indexation for the minimum wage, which was changed again early in 1995. Similar indexation mechanisms should be implemented in other countries. In this regard, we observed that the erosion of the minimum wage had been the most important where the minimum wage had been irregularly adjusted through a tripartite consultation process such as in Bulgaria or Romania. The adaptation of the minimum wage in Hungary in 1993 provides an additional example. As a result of the rise in February 1993, the ratio of the minimum wage to the average wage increased from 33% to 38.8% in the first quarter of 1993, although it fell to 34.6% in the second quarter and further decreased over the following months.

In contrast, such an erosion has been less pronounced when some automatic compensation for inflation has been implemented, as in Poland where the authorities succeeded in maintaining the purchasing power of the minimum wage. We thus see that with rapid price increases in the transition period, the level of the minimum wage with regard to the average wage could not be maintained without a process of indexation, and that a tripartite process is necessary, if not sufficient.[62] Such an indexation

---

[62] This was the main reason for the 1970 reform of the minimum wage system in France. Despite regular adjustments during the 1960s and 1970s, its level relative to average wages

mechanism still does not exist in most countries of Central and Eastern Europe. Such an indexation mechanism is particularly needed in countries with hyperinflation, such as Russia, where inflation was more than 2,000% in 1992, and in Ukraine, where inflation reached an astonishing 10,000% in 1993. Inflation remained high in both countries in 1994. In these two countries, as well as in the Republic of Moldova and the Czech Republic, a system of indexation of the minimum wage was introduced by law, but never enforced. In the short term, the only remedy against a fall in the minimum wage in real terms, where hyperinflation still prevails, is minimum wage indexation. However, in the longer term, while minimum wage indexation should be retained in order to compensate for inflation, it will be necessary to utilise more macroeconomic means of fighting inflation, such as the control of credit.

Further, in those countries where the fall of the minimum wage relative to the average wage has been particularly severe, a stage by stage increase of the minimum wage at a rate above inflation should also be planned. This is particularly needed in Russia in order to adjust the minimum wage progressively towards the minimum level of subsistence. The main aim of this policy should be the reduction of poverty. A generally applicable lower limit should be set in order to protect workers in all industries against inconceivably low wages. The modalities of indexation should also be adapted to the economic and social context. The higher the inflation rate, the more regularly should adjustments be made in order to limit the fall in minimum and average wages in real terms. The period of implementation of the indexation system might also vary by country. Indexation mechanisms in some countries could be implemented on a temporary basis. For instance, the Tripartite Council in Hungary might wish to propose some wage indexation mechanism to accompany the liberalisation of energy prices in 1995; this might be expected to lead to inflationary pressure from which real wages could suffer if no indexation is introduced. Probably, more long–term indexation is needed in countries such as Russia and Ukraine to protect the populace from persistent high inflation.

The period of indexation which is taken into account for indexing wages also brings different results. Wages can be indexed to past inflation or to forecast inflation. The advantage of the first method is that wages are indexed to the real price growth in the economy. Its disadvantage is that it

declined with fewer and fewer workers being covered. The new indexation approach, symbolised by the fixing of the SMIC (inter–occupational minimum growth wage) was intended 'to transform completely the static notion of ensuring for the most disadvantaged a subsistence minimum into a dynamic approach affording them guaranteed and regularly growing participation in the fruits of economic progress'. M. Fontanet in the National Assembly on 10 December 1969, as quoted in 'Le Salaire', in Liaisons Sociales, Supp. No. 7150, Paris, Oct. 1975.

generally takes place after a considerable delay, since the calculation of the inflation rate requires time. One of the ways to avoid this problem is to attempt to adapt wages to inflation several times a year, for instance on a quarterly basis.

The second method, which consists in indexing wages to forecast inflation, allows wages to be immediately adjusted to future price growth. However, official forecasts are generally well below real inflation rates, so that wages are in reality not fully indexed. A compensation mechanism allowing wages to be readjusted according to the difference between the forecast and real inflation rates thus needs to be introduced in the second type of indexation mechanism. However, this compensation mechanism, which is generally negotiated between government, employer and worker representatives who rarely agree on inflation figures, requires a long time before workers are compensated, if at all, for higher than expected inflation. We have seen that different methods have been implemented in Central and Eastern Europe.

Poland introduced a combination of the two systems, with quarterly adjustment according to past and anticipated changes in the consumer price index. In Bulgaria, the government decided in 1994 to change the indexation system based on past inflation to one based on forecast inflation, despite strong trade union opposition. This second method can be extremely disadvantageous in economies where very high and unpredictable inflation rates prevail, such as in Russia and Ukraine. The system of indexation according to forecast inflation would seem to be more appropriate where more modest inflation rates can be more easily anticipated.

(ii) Adapting the minimum wage to the sectoral and regional context

While the emerging and thus imperfect labour markets justify establishing a floor for the wage structure, there are several economic constraints on the level at which this floor can be fixed, considering the difficult economic conditions of some branches and enterprises and their incapacity to pay wages above certain levels. If set at a level having a major impact on the existing wage structure and the average level of wages, there could be unwelcome economic repercussions in the form of increased unemployment, reduced growth and an acceleration of inflation.

Although Buchtikova's study of the Czech Republic (Chapter 6) shows that the increase of the prevailing minimum wage would not have a large adverse effect on employment, it also shows that some industries would have more problems than others in raising the minimum wage, and that the effect on employment could be much greater in those branches. A large increase in the minimum wage could only be achieved by stages in those industries. This means that at the national level the minimum wage should not be set much above the subsistence level, at least initially, and that a complementary process should be worked out at the branch and regional levels.

Although all industries would not be allowed to establish a minimum wage below the national level, trade unions and employer representatives could adapt the minimum wage to the conditions of the *sector*, so allowing the most profitable branches and enterprises to accelerate this process, while giving more time to the others.[63]

Great social and economic differences between *regions* also emphasise the need to complement any minimum wage fixing mechanisms at the national level by a complementary approach at the regional level. On the social side, important regional differences in the subsistence minimum, as in Russia, demonstrate a need to adjust the regional minimum wage to those differences. On the economic side, employers and trade unions in the richest regions could agree on a minimum wage much higher than the national average. Some regions in Russia have already introduced a regional minimum wage that takes into account the value of the subsistence minimum within the region. Such pilot tripartite agreements, between employers' representatives, trade unions and local authorities, were concluded in early 1993 in the regions of Moscow and St Petersburg. Similar regional level agreements might be envisaged in other countries. Although this complementary bargaining process at the regional level appears to be particularly needed in large countries such as Russia and Ukraine, it might also be considered by smaller countries where substantial regional differences in minimum living standards still prevail.

This combination of negotiations at the national, sectoral and regional levels could help the minimum wage to fulfil its social and economic roles. While the national level would help to ensure all workers a basic minimum, and help to protect the most vulnerable groups in the current period of reform, negotiations at more decentralised levels could adapt the minimum wage to economic performance and productivity improvements. This latter economic role could be more important than what is normally foreseen. In economies where wages are still partly determined through state subsidies to specific industries or regions, and so disconnected from economic performance, a minimum wage fixed through tripartite consultation at the national level and then adapted to the prevailing economic and social conditions of the industry and region could probably introduce market mechanisms in the wage determination process and ensure better social protection. Regional bargaining seems to be particularly important in countries such as Russia and Ukraine where substantial regional differences

[63] For details on procedures for fixing minimum wages by industries, regions or categories of workers, see Starr, 1981, op. cit.

between subsistence minimums still prevail. Through regional wage bargaining, the minimum wage in some regions should be increased above the national minimum wage in order better to reflect local economic conditions and, in particular, local price increases. Sectoral bargaining is also an important complementary process in countries such as Bulgaria and Russia where large sectoral differences still prevail, with employers in some sectors being able to fix—through negotiations with trade unions—sectoral minimum wages well above the national level. Through this process, minimum wages would also promote collective bargaining and lessen the pressure on governments to use the minimum wage to control wage movements.

It is interesting that in Estonia, after the adoption of a *Law on Collective Agreements* in April 1993, more than 374 collective agreements (involving 127,900 workers) had been signed by August 1993 and half of them provided for a minimum wage higher than the official level of 300 kroons. Negotiations and the fixing of minimum wages at decentralised levels might also facilitate wage differentiation by sectors, occupations or regions. However, the social partners should negotiate how these different levels of wage bargaining should be combined, and how contradictions between regional and sectoral minimum wage bargaining levels may be avoided. They should also agree on how negotiations on one level should be reflected in negotiations at other levels. For instance, the social partners could agree that a minimum wage decided at the regional level should be implemented by all enterprises and sectors operating in that region. At the same time, they could also agree that a sectoral minimum wage should be applied in all enterprises belonging to that sector, and that regional negotiations would only constitute a complementary process. The prevalence of the regional or sectoral level and their complementarity would depend on national, regional and sectoral specificities, as well as the different bargaining positions of the social partners at the different levels.

(iii) Improving wages in the budget sector

The indexation of the minimum wage would also allow wages in the public sector to rise on a more regular basis and thus improve worker motivation. Because of the financial problems faced in the budget (public) sector, some economists have proposed a dual system, with the minimum wage in the budget sector being fixed at a lower level than in the non–budgetary sector. This proposal may be attractive, private firms having more funds to pay higher rates. Most employees of the public sector have been paid well below the national minimum in Russia and in some other countries. The fact that some governments used the financial problems in the budgetary sector to freeze the national minimum wage also demonstrates the advantages of the dual system. Yet the erosion of real wages has been so strong in the public sector that it would be difficult to justify fixing the minimum wage at lower rates in this sector. Apart from equity considerations, this dual system could also have adverse efficiency implications. Jobs in some parts of the sector, such as health and education, are not only important for society as a whole, but also require high qualifications and skills. Increased wage differentiation would lead to a lack of motivation of employees in the public sector and induce them to leave for the private sector. This wage differentiation as practised in Western countries has led to major strikes and to a lack of qualified employees, a phenomenon particularly felt in the education and health sectors. In this regard, a single national minimum wage that can be reached in the budgetary sector while being increased through additional negotiations between unions and employers in the non–budgetary sector might appear a more equitable and efficient system.[64]

(iv) Disconnecting social benefits from the minimum wage

To the extent that they determine the level of social benefits, government authorities have been reluctant to raise the minimum wage because of its financial implications. This link implied in some countries a reduction in the rate at which minimum wages were increased. This was the case in Estonia, where the minimum wage was not increased for more than two years. This also led to some strange situations, as in Russia where the minimum monthly pension and the average monthly pension in 1992 and 1993 were above the minimum wage. In a context of growing unemployment and of increasing problems for financing unemployment benefits, this situation will not improve. The example of Poland shows that it became possible to increase the minimum wage only after disconnecting unemployment and other social benefits from it. A similar reform is needed in other countries and would have many advantages. While adjusting the minimum wage to inflation and using it as the starting minimum for the whole wage fixing process, it would prevent the government from cutting social benefits through minimum wage negotiations.

Of course, there will be a risk of fragmentation between 'insiders' and 'outsiders', with wages and minimum wages following inflation and nominal social benefits remaining constant. Trade unions will have a delicate role to play, by negotiating the two issues separately while maintaining the purchasing power not only of the minimum wage but of social benefits as well.

---

[64] In order to improve productivity in the budget sector, a reform of the wage determination system in the sector would probably be needed, with the introduction of payment systems linked to individual and collective performance. Such schemes were introduced for instance in France; see M. Rocard: 'Pour la modernisation de l'État', *Revue des Deux Mondes*, 1989.

11. Conclusion

One must stress the importance of collective bargaining for adapting minimum wages to the current worsening social situation, while reflecting the difficult economic conditions. Through a learning process, in a context characterised by emerging employers' associations and a multiplication in the number of trade unions, a statutory minimum wage might constitute an important opportunity for employers and unions to promote and develop industrial relations, to measure together the economic and social problems associated with their current move to a free market economy and to fix an incomes policy that could appropriately respond to these problems.

The role of *trade unions* in this process needs to be strengthened. While the priority on the minimum wage issue must remain the implementation of . mechanisms of indexation, they will have to develop and strengthen their bargaining position at the sectoral and regional levels, and be ready to negotiate minimum wages at these decentralised levels. In this perspective, they will have to collect information on the cost of living, and on the most vulnerable groups, calculate the subsistence minimum at the regional level, and help in identifying the financial and economic potential and performance of the branch or the region.

The role of *employers* is crucial at the different levels of collective bargaining, not only at the sectoral or regional levels, but also within the enterprise, for helping to fix a minimum wage that reflects the financial and economic conditions of the industry, region or enterprise, while covering as far as possible local subsistence needs and helping to avoid workers' demotivation and adverse effects on productivity. Profitable enterprises should also be made aware of the potential benefits of moving the minimum wage upwards as a means of improving productivity and overall competitiveness, and to adapt it to their social and economic conditions.

Nevertheless, this would not be possible without *governments* reconsidering their restrictive tax–based incomes policy to limit the rise in nominal wages and in controlling inflation. Not only has the 'shock therapy' policy led to serious social tensions, due to the fall of the purchasing power of both the average wage and the minimum wage, but it has also prevented the wage mechanism performing an incentive and productivity–enhancing role.[65]

In this context, progressive decentralisation of the wage fixing process might allow wages to perform as a mechanism for raising labour efficiency

[65] For an analysis of such effects in Russia, see G. Standing: 'Wages and work motivation in the Soviet labour market: Why a BIP, not a TIP is required', *International Labour Review*, 1991; for Bulgaria, see ILO-CEET, 1993, op.cit.

and work motivation. An appropriate minimum wage policy could contribute to this process and avoid competitive managerial strategies based on lowering wages rather than technological and product innovation. Through the maintenance of workers' wage purchasing power, this might also boost consumption and production and limit the shift to the informal economy, thus reconciling economic and social objectives.

Appendix:
Changes in the Level of the Minimum Wage

Hungary (HUF)

Date	Level
Jan-88	3 000
Mar-89	3 700
Oct-89	4 000
Feb-90	4 800
Sep-90	5 600
Dec-90	5 800
Apr-91	7 000
Jan-92	8 000
Feb-93	9 000
Feb-94	10 500
Feb-95	12 200

Russia (roubles)

Date	Level
1981	70
Apr-91	130
Jan-92	342
Jun-92	900
Feb-93	2 250
Apr-93	4 275
Aug-93	7 740
Dec-93	14 620
Jul-94	20 500
Apr-95	44 700

Czech Republic (CSK)

Date	Level
Feb-91	2 000
Jan-92	2 200

Romania (lei)

Date	Level
1992	17 600
Jun-93	30 000
Sep-93	40 200
Dec-93	45 000
Mar-94	60 000
Jul-94	65 000

Bulgaria (levs)

Date	Level
Sep-90	191
Jan-91	235
Feb-91	435
Apr-91	518
Jul-91	620
Jul-92	850
Mar-93	1 200
Jul-93	1 343
Oct-93	1 414
Jan-94	1 565

Poland (ZL)

Date	Level
Jan-89	17 800
Jul-89	22 100
Oct-89	38 000
Jan-90	120 000
Sep-90	368 000
Oct-90	440 000
Jan-91	550 000
Apr-91	605 000
Jul-91	632 000
Oct-91	652 000
Dec-91	700 000
Jan-92	875 000
May-92	1 000 000
Aug-92	1 200 000
Sep-92	1 300 000
Oct-92	1 350 000
Jan-93	1 500 000
Jul-93	1 650 000
Oct-93	1 750 000
Jan-94	1 950 000
Apr-94	2 050 000

Albania (leks)

Date	Level
Aug-92	675
Jan-93	840
Jun-93	925
Dec-93	2 400
Oct-94	2 620

Estonia

Date	Level	
Dec-89	70	(roubles)
Feb-90	100	
Jan-91	135	
Jul-91	200	
Jan-92	410	
Feb-92	600	
Mar-92	1 000	
Jul-92	200	(kroons)
Oct-92	300	

Republic of Moldova

Date	Level	
Jan-91	70	(roubles)
Mar-91	100	
Apr-91	165	
Jan-92	400	
Apr-92	850	
Nov-92	1 700	
Mar-93	3 000	
Jun-93	7 500	
Nov-93	10 000	
Jan-94	13.50	(leu)
Jun-94	18	

Ukraine (karbovanets)

Date	Level
Oct-90	80
Oct-91	185
Dec-91	400
May-92	900
Nov-92	2,300
Jan-93	4,600
Jun-93	6,900
Aug-93	20,000
Dec-93	60,000

3

Minimum Wages in Russia: Fantasy Chasing Fact

Tatyana Chetvernina*

1. The Concept

The minimum wage and salary in post–totalitarian Russia are specific concepts derived from the former Soviet Union. In most societies, three primary objectives govern the introduction or maintenance by the State of a minimum wage.

- First, out of a need for social protection with regard to the lower limit of the value of manpower ('protection against exploitation');
- Second, with the purpose of satisfying and maintaining the minimum material and social requirements ('the principle of human dignity');
- Third, in order to promote 'dynamic efficiency', that is obliging enter prises to improve labour productivity rather than pursue a 'cheap labour' policy.

Regrettably it is impossible to call modern Russia a normal society. Under the tightly and centrally regulated conditions of the former Soviet Union, the system of remuneration was based on the universal *Tariff Schedule of Wages and Salaries*.[1] What was called 'the minimum wage' in this schedule corresponded to the remuneration for the simplest, unskilled labour; legally, it was impossible to earn less than envisaged by the Schedule. The Schedule also established the upper wage limit for the most complex, skilled, labour. Legally, it was impossible to earn more than what was stipulated by the Schedule.

As national per capita income increased, and as a consequence of inflation both open and concealed, wage rates and salaries were periodically adjusted upwards. One would expect that, in the event of an increase in the minimum wage, all other tariffs and salaries, pensions, scholarships and social benefits would be calculated accordingly and increased pro rata. In fact, the entire schedule shifted to a higher level. Moreover, wage rates and salaries were recalculated and most coefficients were introduced

* Centre for Labour Market Studies, Institute of Economics, Russian Academy of Sciences, Moscow.
[1] This schedule was applied to different regions and sectors with the help of many supplements and coefficients, which rendered the system of remuneration relatively flexible but utterly muddled.

on an arbitrary basis, depending on particular preferences given to different spheres and types of labour, sectors and regions.[2]

Until the 1970s, the minimum wage in the Soviet Union took account of the real minimum needed for subsistence. In 1968, minimum wages in all sectors of the national economy were raised from 40 or 45 roubles to 60 roubles per month. Whereas in 1965 the average wage amounted to 96.5 roubles, in 1970 it was 122 roubles. Artificial pricing made it possible to maintain relatively stable prices for essential goods, while so-called public consumption funds financed universal free education and medical services (admittedly, of varying quality for different groups of the population), and housing and transport costs were relatively small, even for low-income groups. In other words, we may say that the minimum wage was not far from the minimum of material security. In effect it corresponded to the Soviet standard of living in the 1960s and 1970s.

The mid-1970s saw a gradual transition to a new minimum wage level— 70 roubles a month. In 1974, the average wage was 141.1 roubles and in 1978 it was 160 roubles. In 1981, the 26th CPSU Congress declared that the Government would raise the minimum wage to 80 roubles a month, but the Communist Party failed to keep its promise. The minimum wage of 70 roubles a month was maintained up to 1 April 1991 and, of course, by that time had lost its connection with the living wage. For instance, in 1989 the average wage was 158.6 roubles, while the subsistence minimum came to 135 roubles; in 1990, the respective figures were 296.8 and 144 roubles.

However, in the 1970s, for most workers providing simple, unskilled labour, the actual wage was higher than the established minimum wage. In the 1980s, there were very few workers whose incomes were limited by this minimum. First, this was due to the almost general application of additions and ratios and, since 1966, due to payments from the material incentive funds established in each enterprise. Second, the Soviet economy was built on the widespread use of unskilled labour. From the early 1970s, the country had a growing deficit of unskilled labour and for this reason in the 1980s unskilled workers performed their jobs for a wage corresponding to more complex tasks; working pensioners also retained their pensions, while those who worked overtime often had two or three workplaces.

Thus, the concept of minimum wage in the Soviet Union was gradually detached from the requirements of social protection. On the one hand, the purchasing power of the minimum wage, even taking account of additions and ratios, could not be compared with the cost of labour. On the other, the authorities did not need to raise the minimum wage, since the

[2] For instance, the salaries of university teachers were unchanged between the 1960s and the end of the 1980s, whereas average wages rose by roughly 2.5 times during this period.

real incomes of all groups of the active population were substantially higher than the fixed minimum and approached the average wage. The average wage began to play the role of the minimum fixed as the living wage. This is clear from table 3.1, compiled on the basis of incomes received by two average families, one consisting of three persons, in which two members worked for an average wage, the other consisting of four persons, two of whom were working for an average wage.

Table 3.1 *Wages and Family Income, Soviet Union, 1989–90 (roubles)*

Year	Average wage	Family income*	Income per person		Living wage
			family of 3	family of 4	
1989	258.6	447	149	112	135
1990	296.8	507	169	127	144

* Including taxes and other mandatory deductions.
Source: GOSKOMSTAT.

In the family consisting of four members with two working, the average wages did not ensure a subsistence minimum. It is not surprising that in most regions of the Soviet Union, according to several sources, the number of families with two or more children steadily diminished.

In other words, the average income roughly corresponded to the minimum living wage. Hence, the section of the population whose incomes were below average did not obtain a subsistence minimum. For this reason, the statistical bodies did not publish data on the subsistence minimum in the press.

After 1 April 1991 all workers and other employees began to receive 'compensation' of 60 roubles a month to make up for the sharp rise in prices set in train by the Pavlov Government. In this way, the minimum wage in the Soviet Union came to 130 roubles a month. But this compensation was insufficient. In 1991, prices for most consumer goods doubled or trebled. Towards the end of 1991, when the estimated subsistence minimum was 200 roubles, the real subsistence minimum was 700 roubles per month. This supports our conclusion that in the last days of the Soviet Union the minimum wage could not be compared with the subsistence minimum and had long ceased to be an instrument of social protection.

In fact, the socio–economic content of the minimum wage in the new Russia has remained the same as in the old Soviet Union. Moreover, it would be senseless to expect an approximation of the minimum wage to the living wage in conditions of declining production and the relatively tough monetarist policy of the Yeltsin Government. Just as in the former Soviet Union, the average wage, not the minimum wage, makes possible an existence close to a subsistence minimum. Even after the failure of monetarist policy, there is no real link between the minimum wage and the subsistence minimum, as was the case before. We go into this topic in greater detail below.

Strictly speaking, in Russia today the concept of minimum wage first of all denotes the basic unit used for calculating salaries (tariff rates) according to the single rate schedule (SRS) employed in enterprises, organisations and institutions financed from the budget. Introduced in December 1992, the SRS provides for 18 rates (categories). The minimum rate corresponds to the first category; the amount paid to the other grades being determined by multiplying the minimum rate by the ratio provided for the respective category (table 3.2). For example, in January 1993, the minimum rate was 1,800 roubles. Hence, a doctor or teacher certified according to the 10th category received 7,182 roubles (1,800 x 3.99).

Table 3.2 *The Single Rate Schedule, Russia, 1993*

Rate	Ratio	Rate	Ratio
1 -	1.00	10 -	3.99
2 -	1.30	11 -	4.51
3 -	1.69	12 -	5.10
4 -	1.91	13 -	5.76
5 -	2.16	14 -	6.51
6 -	2.44	15 -	7.36
7 -	2.76	16 -	8.17
8 -	3.12	17 -	9.07
9 -	3.53	18 -	10.07

Source: GOSKOMSTAT.

The SRS rate is established in the following way. Once every few months, irregularly, Parliament or the President introduces a new minimum wage. This entails that the SRS minimum rate automatically rises to the level of a new minimum wage. On the basis of the *Decree of the President of Russia*, the Government may establish a higher, but not a lower, SRS minimum rate. For instance, in February and March 1993 the SRS minimum rate and the minimum wage coincided at 2,250 roubles. From 1 April 1993 the Parliament established the minimum wage at a level of 4,275 roubles, while the President and the Government fixed the SRS minimum rate at a level of 4,500 roubles. Thus, a situation may develop, when two minima will operate: one in the extra–budget sphere and the second—higher than the first—only in the budget sphere. In August 1994 there was a greater difference between the national minimum wage (20,500) and the SRS minimum rate in the budgetary sector (22,000).

The situation is complicated further by the fact that, in reality, the minimum wage is guaranteed only in the budget sphere (SRS minimum rate).

Enterprises not financed from budgetary sources introduce a new minimum wage only when they obtain financial resources for the purpose, which may be several months after the new rate comes into effect under the law. These extra–budgetary enterprises can be divided into two groups:

- In those working more or less normally even the most unskilled worker is paid substantially above the minimum wage; in some branches, the average wage exceeds by dozens of times the established minimum, and here wage rises take place regardless of the minimum amount.
- In those that are on the verge of bankruptcy the introduction of a new minimum wage is, as a rule, delayed until the end of the statutory term. Soon after this, the lawmaker establishes a higher minimum wage, but its actual introduction is also likely to be postponed. Therefore, enterprises are able legally to violate the right of citizens to receive a minimum wage and so avoid bankruptcy.

Further, the minimum wage is used as the basic unit for calculating the minimum social benefits not associated with labour activity. The minimum unemployment benefit is equal to the minimum wage, and in practice it seems most registered unemployed receive that amount.[3] Scholarships are paid on the strength of the minimum wage in the following amounts: not less than 100% to postgraduate students, not less than 80% to students of higher educational establishments, and not less than 70% to students of secondary educational establishments. If the monthly income for one member of the family is below the minimum wage, then such a family is regarded as low–income and has the right to receive social assistance.

Finally, with inflation at 2,500% in 1992, 1,000% in 1993 and 300% in 1994, the concept of minimum wage serves as a unit of measurement for calculating fines, state duties and dues, income subject to taxation, etc. For instance, it is used to calculate income tax since income subject to taxation does not include the minimum wage. For certain groups, such as invalids, the nontaxable part of their income is defined as several times the minimum wage. The wage–fund tax is not levied on enterprises and organisations whose average wage does not exceed four times the minimum wage.[4] If their average wage exceeds this amount, differential tax rates are applied.

To sum up, we can say that in the Russia of today the minimum wage is a multipurpose notion. It is a universal unit of measurement applicable for the computation of monetary benefits, particularly those not connected with remuneration. The minimum wage has increased along with inflation and for this reason it is more convenient in legislative terms to operate on

[3] G. Standing (1994): 'Why is unemployment so low in Russia: The net with many holes', *Journal of European Social Policy*, Vol. 4, No. 1. This is based on a survey of jobseekers in 18 districts, carried out in 1993.

[4] The wage–fund tax is a variant of the tax–based incomes policy first introduced as the 'Abalkin tax'.

the basis of sums expressed, not in absolute monetary terms, but with reference to the 'minimum wage'. And since the minimum wage does not provide a subsistence income, it must be admitted that its basic function is to serve as the equivalent of a monetary sum with a relatively constant purchasing capacity. This function is conditioned by the extremely high rate of inflation in Russia, and so cannot last.

2. The Minimum Wage and the Living Wage

During 1992, production in Russia fell by roughly 20%. It was therefore to be expected that the former average wage and average income per capita would no longer apply, and that they would not guarantee a subsistence minimum calculated according to Soviet standards. Because of inflation and delays in adjusting the minimum wage, it has become substantially less than the average monthly wage. Since the minimum wage is recalculated irregularly, in some months of 1992 and 1993 it was less than one–tenth of the average. In December 1992, the average was 17.9 times the minimum wage and in January 1993 it was 17.4 times. Meanwhile, as a result of greatly increased social differentiation, the number of people whose per capita income is less than a quarter of the average income has risen substantially. No wonder government agencies have twice reviewed the concept of the subsistence minimum.

For instance, since 1992, the subsistence minimum in the old, Soviet sense of the word has been known as 'the minimum consumer budget'. Trade unions designate this concept the 'normative subsistence minimum'. The normative minimum is calculated according to average prices, and includes foodstuffs and consumer goods, i.e. social benefits that make it possible to exist without risk to physical health and mental functioning. In 1992 and 1993, the average monthly wage fluctuated around the normative minimum, depending on the rate of inflation.[5] For example, their correlation in Moscow is presented in table 3.3, according to data supplied by the Moscow Trade Union Federation.

It is important to emphasise that the Russian normative minimum is far from what is included in the normative minimum as calculated in developed market economies. The cost of the normative minimum in Russia, even at the relatively low Russian prices, comprised 49,449 roubles in November 1992 and 63,731 roubles (USD 110) in December 1992, or five times more than the Russian normative minimum.[6]

[5] Since November 1992, there have been no official data on the normative minimum ('minimum consumer budget'), as government agencies have refused to make use of this concept.

[6] *Kommersant*, No. 2, 1993, p. 18.

Table 3.3 *Normative Minimum and Average Wage, Moscow, 1992–93 (roubles)*

	1992			1993		
	March	June	November	December	January	February
Normative minimum	2 884	4 662	6 442	14 034	19 184	23 577
Average monthly wage	2 153	4 268	6 775	15 454	15 998	18 996

Source: GOSKOMSTAT.

What is officially termed the 'subsistence minimum' is called by the Moscow trade unions the 'physiological minimum'. It is based on the lowest quality, lowest-priced food items and reflects the lowest acceptable conditions for sustaining health and a beggarly existence.

The physiological minimum is calculated by the Ministry of Labour of the Russian Federation. The first calculation method was introduced on 16 April 1992. According to this, the physiological minimum amounted to:

–   1,759 roubles in April 1992, when the minimum wage was 342 roubles;
–   2,341 roubles in June 1992, when the minimum wage was 900 roubles;
–   2,963 roubles in September, when the minimum wage was 900 roubles.

By the summer of 1992, the absurdity of the minimum wage level was clear for all to see. Why should we call this unit of measurement the 'minimum wage', if its value is less than a third of the physiological minimum. In this situation, one would expect the State to bring the minimum wage closer to the physiological minimum: in Russia just the opposite happened.

The Ministry of Labour admitted that it had been too extravagant when it approved the abovementioned calculation method in April 1992. In order to correspond to the state of the Russian economy in November 1992, the Ministry of Labour elaborated a new method for calculating the physiological

Table 3.4 *Physiological Minimum Income, Russia, Jan 1992–Mar 1993 (roubles)*

	1992			1993		
	January	May	June	January	February	March
Physiological min. according to the method of 16 April 1992	907	2 008	2 341	8 534	-	-
Minimum according to the method of 10 Nov 1992	635	1 405	1 639	5 353	~ 6 800	~ 8 000
Minimum wage	342	342	900	900	2 250	2 250

Source: GOSKOMSTAT.

minimum. It reasoned as follows: in normal conditions a Russian citizen has to spend a definite sum of money per month in order not to die from hunger, but in the economic crisis he needed to spend much less in order to avoid starvation. For instance, the 'critical' norms of nourishment were lowered, allowing for the consumption of 27.5 kilograms of meat by one person a year, including 700 grams of sausages, instead of the previous minimum level of 54 kilograms. Meanwhile, the minimum wage level remained below the 'critical physiological minimum' (table 3.4).

It is impossible to forecast to what extent the gap will be maintained between the subsistence minimum and the minimum wage. From 1993 on, the parliament and the relevant government agencies have spoken increasingly of the need to give a social dimension to economic reform. Towards the end of 1992, the leadership of the Ministry of Labour changed and its attitude to the concept of minimum wage was modified. In the words of outgoing Deputy Minister Vladimir Kosmarsky, the gap between the minimum wage and the subsistence minimum was 'not the result of somebody's malicious intention, but a direct and inevitable consequence of the chronic troubles of the Russian economy. The country, which could be classified by many indicators as a Third World country, is unable to guarantee to all people an income not lower than the subsistence minimum, for this is the privilege only of developed societies.'[7]

The new Ministry of Labour officials dealing with the issue prepared a draft proposal, adopted on 23 March 1993 as the *President's Decree on Urgent Measures to Stabilise the Standard of Living of the Population of the Russian Federation of 1993*. On this subject, the Decree merely states: 'The subsistence minimum shall be used as a social indicator to guide the stage–by–stage improvement of the minimum wage.' In fact, it was no more than a declaration of intent.

The minimum wage was raised in April 1993 to 4,275 roubles. In the budget sphere the minimum salary was increased to 4,500 roubles. According to my estimates, based on their method, the 'critical physiological minimum' was then 10,000 roubles, and in May 1993 it was 13,000 roubles.[8]

It is also necessary to note here that a rise in the minimum wage to a level near to the physiological minimum would lead to a revision of the payment system in the budget sphere. Otherwise it would turn into a major factor of inflation. We will deal with this problem in more detail later.

---

[7] *Segodnya* (Moscow), 27 April 1993.

[8] According to the new Law on the Minimum Wage Rate of 13 November 1992 the minimum wage had to be increased every quarter from 1 April. However, although the minimum wage was increased in the first, second and third quarters its increase in the fourth quarter was postponed to December (table 3.5). Again, in 1994, the minimum wage was not increased in the first and second quarters, but only in July 1994 to 20,500, so that it reached 24% of the subsistence minimum—84,100 roubles (table 3.5).

3. The Minimum Wage and Incomes

In March 1993, the minimum wage was 2,250 roubles. According to data supplied by the Russian State Statistics Committee, about 10% of the population had a per capita income less than twice the minimum wage. These are people who live far below the poverty level. Another 27% of the population had incomes ranging from two to four minimum wages. Thus, over one–third of Russia's population lived poorly. Nearly a quarter of the population had incomes ranging from four to six minimum wages, 15% had incomes from six to eight minimum wages, and about 23% eight minimum wages or more.

In this connection, consider the process of social stratification. According to the official statistics on registered income, by December 1992 the index of concentration of the current pecuniary income of the population (the Gini coefficient) was 0.327, up from 0.256 in 1991, and the difference between the income of the richest 10% of the population and the poorest 10% had risen to 8.7 times, having been 45.4 times in 1991.

We may suppose that in reality the gap between the incomes of the poor and those of the rich is much greater. First, a sizeable part of the Russian economy is associated with illegal, often criminal activity; second, part of the income of the richest finds its way abroad; and third, there are numerous possibilities for concealing income from the tax authorities at a time when a new tax system is in the process of formation. The richest stratum of society is just one group on whose income official statistics can provide no information. The wealthy account for only a few per cent of the population, but their incomes are measured by thousands of minimum wages. In the opinion of officials from the Ministry of Economics, State Statistics Committee data have underestimated the absolute average income level by 15 to 20%.[9] For the richest stratum the underestimate must therefore be enormous.

The gap in income between rich and poor is also subject to great regional variation.[10] The most conspicuous gap is in the North Caucasus, where the difference has been 20–22 times.

Such substantial social differentiation is a new phenomenon in our society and unacceptable to a population spoon–fed on egalitarian sloganeering for seventy years. The difference in income between the poorest and richest is an important political factor, which indirectly influences changes in the minimum wage. It is often mentioned when the

[9]   Russia is divided into 'rich' regions, such as Moscow City or Nizhni Novgorod, and 'poor' regions, such as Ivanovo, *Izvestia* (Moscow), 13 February 1993, p. 2.
[10]   Regions are understood to mean the components of the Russian Federation and its administrative–territorial units.

Government and the parliament fix new minimum wage levels, often competing for popular attention.[11]

Regional income differentiation is another problem. Economic reform is being pursued in a vast country inhabited by many nationalities living in social and political instability. There are many economic and extra–economic factors, relating both to the past and the present, as a result of which Russia has neither a single consumer market nor a single socio–economic area. In such conditions, there arise substantial income gaps between regions and differences in the value of the subsistence minimum.

Thus, in December 1992, the maximum gap between average wages in different regions was 11 times and in per capita terms it was 12.7 times. These are maximum figures, but the average per capita income in 'poor' and 'rich' regions differed roughly by 5 times. As for the regional subsistence minima, their sizes differ by 2 or 3 times.[12]

Therefore, 'low' and 'very low' incomes in various regions are estimated in different ways. Speaking conditionally, if the average subsistence minimum in Russia equals four minimum wages, this means that in one region it is equal to two minimum wages, and in another six or seven. Thus, if the Federal authorities increased the uniform wage minimum in Russia by four times, this would be 'very good' for some regions and have little effect in others. Local authorities in 'rich' regions can supplement the Federal minimum wage at the expense of local budgets.

It is therefore highly questionable whether the minimum wage should be uniform for the whole of Russia while such regional differences persist. Below we consider this question in more detail.

We must emphasise further that the minimum wage has not so far exerted any perceptible influence on the dynamic of the average monthly wage in the national economy.[13] Thus, from April to December 1992, the average monthly wage rose from 3,052 to 16,071 roubles, while the minimum wage remained at 900 roubles. In January 1993, the average wage fell to 15,690 roubles, although the minimum wage was unchanged.[14]

---

[11] For instance, in March 1993 Parliament fixed the minimum wage at 4,275 roubles; shortly afterwards the President announced that the minimum salary in the budget sphere would be 4,500 roubles.

[12] As a result of extra–economic factors (e.g. artificial price formation) the subsistence minimum is not always dependent directly on the level of average per capita income in a region. For example, in a 'rich' region retail prices of staple foodstuffs may be lower than in a 'poor' one, due to the distribution of goods according to coupons.

[13] There is only an impact in the nonbudgetary sphere through taxation. The wage fund is taxed when the average wage exceeds 4 times the minimum wage: up to eight minimum wages at 32% and above 8 minimum wages at 50%. Therefore, the wage could be increased after a rise in the minimum wage and result in a lower level of tax payment.

[14] This was due to the fact that in December 1992 the average wage rose sharply (by 50% as compared with November) for end–of–year reasons not connected with enterprise performance.

In February 1993, the minimum wage was raised to 2,250 roubles, or by 150%. But this was in no way reflected in the rate of growth of the average wage: as in 1992 the average wage increased by approximately 20% every month.[15] This testifies to the fact that the monthly growth of the average wage has been determined mainly by continued subsidies given to different sectors of the national economy and the regions. The periodic rise in the SRS minimum rate may also be regarded as a subsidy.

The rising minimum SRS rate does not exert a substantial influence on the growth of the average wage: it is 'lost' in the general mass of subsidies to the national economy. Thus, in September 1992 the minimum salary in the budget sphere rose from 900 to 1,350 roubles (table 3.4). This month witnessed the peak growth in the average wage, 26%. Immediately before this development, the State had written off the debts of loss–making enterprises on a national basis, an indirect subsidy which enabled most enterprises in the nonbudgetary sphere to raise wages.

In December 1992, the minimum SRS rate was fixed at 1,800 roubles, this being accompanied by a leap of the average wage of 50%. But in that month, all enterprises in the extrabudgetary sphere raised wages artificially for a month, because of the attendant tax benefits. In February 1992, the minimum SRS rate was increased to 2,250 roubles, while the minimum wage rose from 900 to 2,250 roubles, but for this reason growth of the average nominal wage was quite normal, 19% in February and 18% in March.

However, we may assume that if the minimum wage approaches the subsistence minimum, the picture of the growth of the average wage will change appreciably. So far, this growth has been determined by the 'rich' regions and economic sectors where today's extremely small minimum wage has shown no growth.

4. Problems and Prospects for the Minimum Wage in Russia

The basic tasks for policymakers include at least the following:

- establishment of a minimum wage closer to the physiological subsistence minimum;
- review of the SRS concept;
- transfer by the Federal authorities of part of the competence for fixing the minimum wage to regional level;
- regulation of the minimum wage by the *General Tariff Agreements* and regional agreements with the participation of trade unions;

[15] As shown in table 3.5, this absence of correlation was also observed in 1993 and 1994, average wages continuing to increase at a regular rate despite the irregular increase in the minimum wage decided in April, July and December 1993 and July 1994.

– consideration of whether, for the transitional period, two minimum wages should be established, one for the state sector, another for the private sector.

Of course, the minimum wage should approach the physiological minimum. If this is impossible today, then at least it is necessary to draft a program for a stage–by–stage increase of the minimum wage at a rate above inflation. Such a programme is planned in the *Draft Law of the Russian Federation on the Subsistence Minimum*, drafted in the spring of 1993, but still not finalised by July.

Achieving a rate of growth higher than the rate of inflation is impossible with the existing SRS single–rate wage schedule. The above principle underlying the SRS concept is that the minimum SRS rate salary in the budgetary sphere may not be below the minimum wage. Yet, if the minimum wage is substantially lower than the subsistence minimum, the rate of the second, third or some higher category may be the lower rate of SRS. In reality, the fifth category has become the base rate, the majority of employees in the budget sphere having rates ranging between the eighth and fifteenth categories, which means that they receive from three to seven times the minimum wage.

Nevertheless, employees in the budgetary sphere have proved to be in a disadvantaged position. The average wage in this sphere is lower than the average wage in the national economy as a whole.[16] Thus, in March 1993 the national average wage was 22,000 roubles, whereas the maximum possible salary in the budgetary sphere, according to the rate of the eighteenth category, was only 22,657 roubles (2,250 x 10.07).[17] In April 1993, the base SRS rate was doubled. The Government claimed that it had found resources for financing all branches of the budgetary sphere debt over several months, but in any case in two or three months inflation would erode the real value of the base SRS rate. Moreover, wage growth in the nonbudgetary sphere, based on subsidies, is the main source of inflation.

The situation would change if the minimum wage approached the subsistence minimum. For this, it would be necessary to increase the minimum wage by three or four times. In the budgetary sphere, the SRS scale would rise proportionately and the average wage in that sphere would be substantially higher than the average wage nationally. Workers would be in a disadvantaged position in the nonbudgetary sphere, where the rise in the

---

[16] There are no exact data on this. For example, it is well–known that in March 1992 the salary in the budget sphere accounted for 50% of the average wage, in December 64%. But it should be 90% in the opinion of the Ministry of Labour. *Trud* (Moscow), 9 June 1993, p. 2.

[17] The salary in government agencies is much higher.

Table 3.5 *Changes in Minimum and Monthly Wages, Russia, January 1992–August 1994 (roubles)*

1992

	I	II	III	IV	V	VI	VII	VIII	IX	X	XI	XII
Average monthly wage in the national economy	1 438	2 004	2 726	3 052	3 675	5 067	5 452	5 876	7 379	8 856	10 057	16 071
Average monthly wage in industry	1 801	2 567	3 470	3 769	4 296	5 948	6 305	6 734	8 140	10 327	12 234	18 400
Minimum wage	342	342	342	342	900	900	900	900	900	900	900	900
Minimum salary in budget sector	342	342	500	500	900	900	900	900	1 350	1 350	1 350	1 800
Minimum pension	342	542	542	642	900	900	900	1 320	1 320	1 320	2 250	2 250
Average monthly pension	438	638	638	738	1 383	1 383	1 383	1 803	1 803	1 803	3 600	3 600
Subsistence minimum	635	774	1 031	1 226	1 405	1 639	1 779	1 939	2 163	2 584	3 285	4 282

1993

	I	II	III	IV	V	VI	VII	VIII	IX	X	XI	XII
Average monthly wage in the national economy	15 690	18 672	22 000	30 500	37 505	47 400	56 000	65 400	80 900	93 000	105 000	130 000
Average monthly wage in industry	-	22 698	-	34 181	39 865	-						
Minimum wage	900	2 250	2 250	4 275	4 275	4 275	4 275	7 740	7 740	7 740	7 740	14 620
Minimum salary in budget sector	1 800	2 250	2 250	4 275	4 275	4 500	4 500	4 500	8 000	8 000	8 000	16 000
Minimum pension	2 250	4 275	4 275	4 275	8 122	8 122	8 122	14 620	14 620	14 620	14 620	14 620
Average monthly pension	-	7 985	-	-	-	-	-	-	-	-	-	-
Subsistence minimum	5 547	6 755	8 069	9 875	12 897	16 527	21 206	24 764	28 193	32 400	37 908	42 800

1994	I	II	III	IV	V	VI	VII	VIII
Average monthly wage in the national economy	134 161	144 700	164 833	171 500	183 500	207 500	221 000	-
Average monthly wage in industry	-	-	-	-	-	-	-	-
Minimum wage	14 620	14 620	14 620	14 620	14 620	14 620	20 500	20 500
Minimum salary in budget sector	16 000	16 000	16 000	16 000	16 000	16 000	22 000	22 000
Minimum pension	14 620	14 620	14 620	14 620	19 000	19 000	19 000	21 850
Average monthly pension	41 800	49 800	49 800	56 000	-	-	-	92 000
Subsistence minimum	47 189	54 759	60 388	66 388	66 536	77 847	84 100	91 800

Source: GOSKOMSTAT

minimum wage would not lead to a corresponding growth in income. The Government would have to increase subsidies many times, and it is not difficult to imagine the inflationary consequences of this development. The minimum wage would be much lower than the subsistence minimum. The uncertified rise of salaries in the budget sphere would give a strong impetus to a revival of the inflationary spiral. With the automatic rise in the minimum SRS rate the average salary in the budgetary sphere would initially be several times higher than the subsistence minimum. Moreover, in absolute terms the people who would have the greatest income growth would be those who already receive the maximum salaries according to the SRS.

Consequently, it is evident that the SRS concept should be revised. It would be possible to fix the minimum SRS rate below the minimum wage. But in this case it is not excluded in principle that employees who have the rates of the lowest categories will receive less than the officially established minimum salary. For this reason, it is necessary to review the number of categories and the increasing coefficients, bearing in mind that the minimum SRS rate will be close to the subsistence minimum. The main objective is to introduce a new category determination system: the rate of the first category, i.e. the base rate of a new SRS, must actually be the lowest rate of the SRS.

This gives rise to a new problem. Although the minimum wage is fixed at national level, the subsistence minimum differs on a regional basis: the obvious corollary of this is that in some regions the minimum wage may fall far short of the subsistence minimum. Consequently, until the considerable regional differences now existing gradually disappear, and a coherent socio–economic area comes into being, the regional authorities have a key role in complementing decisions taken at national level by the federal authorities.

We propose the following expedient, which is being discussed as an aspect of regional policy. The regions themselves should determine their own subsistence minima, proceeding from the regional cost of living and economic potential, with an eye to the specific pattern of regional consumption. After this, the Federal authorities should establish a base national minimum according to the region with the lowest minimum wage. This means that the regional authorities would not be able to establish a minimum wage less than the national minimum, but would be able to set a higher level. This presupposes that such regional minima would not be secured by subsidies from the Federal Government. In the budget sphere, the minimum wage could be guaranteed only at the expense of regional taxes and regional budgets. This requires a proper delimitation of Federal and regional taxes. The taxation system in Russia today does not recognise such a boundary, and until a new Russian Constitution is adopted, the policy expounded here is unrealisable.

Some regions have already introduced a regional minimum wage taking into account the value of the subsistence minimum in the region. This has become possible thanks to the growing activity of regional trade union confederations.

Thus, in February 1993 the Government, trade unions and employer representatives of the city of Moscow concluded a *Tripartite Agreement for 1993*.[18] It provided that the parties determine and publish every quarter the subsistence minimum for Moscow (Item 3.1), while the employers 'guarantee the payment of minimum wages and salaries to workers and other employees for a full working day not below the subsistence minimum. At enterprises where wages are below the subsistence minimum they shall elaborate, together with trade unions, and realise programmes for the approximation of the minimum wage to the subsistence minimum' (Item 3.3).

How this Agreement is implemented in practice is another matter, and by July 1993 no information was available. First, data on the subsistence minimum had not been published in the mass media in Moscow. Therefore, it was not clear which subsistence minimum was meant, normative or physiological. If it was the normative minimum, the Agreement could not be implemented. In March 1993 the average wage in Moscow was about 22,000 roubles while the normative minimum was 28,048 roubles.[19] It seems that the physiological minimum was what they had in mind, and not a 'normal', but a 'critical' one. In March 1993, the 'normal' minimum comprised 14,376 roubles and the 'critical' one 9,564 roubles, while the official minimum wage was 2,250 roubles. Even in March 1993, the minimum wage in Moscow would have been 4.25 times more than the official minimum. Second, it is not clear what stands behind the formulation of trade union demands that there should be a strategy to move the minimum wage towards the subsistence minimum. For instance, in March 1992 the Federation of Independent Trade Unions of Russia (FITUR) assessed the average subsistence minimum in the country at 19,000 roubles. In its talks with the Government on the *General Tariff Agreement*, FITUR insisted that the minimum wage should move closer to the subsistence minimum and demanded that the minimum wage should be fixed on 1 April at 6,000 roubles (32% of 19,000 roubles).[20] But the Government decided on a level of 4,275 roubles asserting that this sum was also 'approaching' the subsistence minimum.

[18] The concept of employer denotes the Moscow Association of Industrialists and Businessmen, which unites enterprises in the nonbudgetary sphere, including the private.

[19] According to the Moscow trade unions.

[20] *Trud* (Moscow), 4 May 1993, p. 2.

The regional minimum wage has been viewed differently in St Petersburg and in the St Petersburg Region. The local trade unions also concluded agreements similar to the *Tripartite Agreement* reached in Moscow. For example, the *Agreement on Socio–economic Policy and the Development of Social Partnership in 1993*, concluded in St Petersburg, stipulated that the regional minimum would be common for all enterprises and organisations, both budgetary and nonbudgetary, and the regional minimum would be at the level of the all–Russian official minimum, with a quarterly correction factor for the excess value of the 'minimum consumer basket' in St Petersburg as against the average in Russia (Item 2.2 of the Agreement). In other words, if the parties to this Agreement asserted that the value of the basic set of social benefits in St Petersburg was 50% higher than the average throughout Russia, then the minimum wage in the city would also be higher than the all–Russian level by 50%. This would be the so–called official minimum wage in St Petersburg; it would be substantially lower than the subsistence minimum in the city, but the local authorities and employers would be obliged to ensure this minimum.

The Agreement also provides that employers must facilitate the establishment of a minimum wage not lower than the subsistence minimum in St Petersburg through collective agreements on basic wage rates, whereas the trade unions must achieve the same result through those agreements (Items 2.7 and 2.8). Analogous provisions are also to be found in the Agreement for the surrounding St Petersburg Region.

Unfortunately, so far there are no data on how this Agreement has been implemented, though the St Petersburg variant of the *Tripartite Agreement* seems preferable to the Moscow one. On the one hand, the parties to the Agreement have not undertaken obviously impractical obligations. The mandatory all–Russian minimum wage will only be 'transformed' into the obligatory one for the whole region at a level which the employers and regional authorities are able to provide. In the budgetary sphere, the salary will be neither excessively high nor inflationary. On the other hand, this does not exclude the possibility that the real minimum wage will guarantee a subsistence minimum in profitable sectors and enterprises.

Hence the following problem. In conditions of economic crisis and transition to a new economic system branches and sectors of the economy that cannot be efficient to an equal degree must coexist. Should the minimum wage in this transitional period be the same for both efficient and nonefficient—that is, private and state (nonbudgetary)—sectors.

At this point, we may revert to the concept of a minimum wage as it pertains to a normal society, and to its function as 'protection from exploitation'. In a normal society, the State is only a minority employer, the main role being played by private employers. For this reason, the State may fix a relatively high minimum wage and compel enterprises to seek their profits through increased efficiency rather than a lowering of the value of labour power. This means that only the most efficient enterprises manage to survive in a competitive market, so stimulating further gains in efficiency, and so on.

Unless the wage system were reformed *in toto*, this scheme could not be applied to present day Russia, since the State and the Federal and regional authorities are still the main employers. If the State established a minimum wage near the subsistence minimum, it would either have to break its promises or intensify stagflation and, most importantly, threaten social stability. Whole sections of the national economy and regions that could not be profitable would be severely hit; the country would suffer even higher unemployment, and economic reform would fail. For this reason, in the current crisis period, the State will tend to fix a low minimum wage and thus understate the cost of labour power. Furthermore the low minimum wage will continue to sustain inefficient and nonrational forms of economic activity, even in the private sector. The only way to break this vicious circle is to reform the wage system by disconnecting the wage structure from the minimum wage concept. Both must be reformed, simultaneously.

By definition, a private sector cannot be unprofitable: if private enterprise exists, it must be making a profit. Consequently, in the emerging private sector the minimum wage must be fixed—through collective bargaining—at a substantially higher level that the existing one, and well above the normative subsistence minimum defined earlier as the minimum basket of goods and services needed for human survival.

Some commentators have argued that the minimum wage issue in the private sector is not important. In the private sector, it is widely believed that wages and salaries are higher than overall average wages and salaries, although there are no available national statistics to demonstrate this. However, according to anecdotal evidence, the situation is not quite so straightforward. Foreign companies operating in Russia seem to pay unskilled labour wages several times the normative subsistence minimum. As a rule, Russian private companies pay high wages only for highly skilled labour. There seem to be many small private businesses in which unskilled labour is paid below the normative minimum. In many societies with reasonable systems of social protection and labour market regulation, such businesses might not remain competitive; yet in Russia they thrive, chiefly at the expense of lowering the cost of labour power. This tendency is becoming stronger as unemployment rises.

Thus, it seems advisable for a specified period of transition, perhaps three years, to have two official all–Russian minimum wages, one for the state, the other for the private sector. If we proceed from the assumption that the minimum wage must sustain the reproduction of labour power, the minimum in the private sector must correspond to the minimum family budget for three persons, two adults and one child. This minimum is approximately two and a half times the normal subsistence minimum for one man. In March 1993, it would have been 30 minimum wages, 2,250 roubles each, and in April roughly 18 minimum wages, 4,275 roubles each. In other words, the minimum wage in the private sector must be higher than in the public sector. As the economic situation in the country improves, the minimum in the public sector could gradually catch up with the minimum in the private sector.

The enforced establishment in the private sector of such a high minimum would ruin most small enterprises whose existence depends upon the lower cost of labour power; on the other hand, it might force them to improve productivity to cover the higher wage costs.

Further, in terms of taxation private enterprises would be in a strong position as compared with state enterprises, since the wage bill is taxed in accordance with the value of the minimum wage, and in the private sector this would be much higher. This would be a further stimulus to the development of an efficient private sector.

Eventually, this would lead to growing employment in the private sector and to an outflow of labour to more efficient economic sectors, create competition to state economic enterprises and so, perhaps, positively influence their efficiency. In short, a dualistic approach would be worth trying, and would be infinitely preferable to the current fantasy of a minimum wage that is nothing of the kind.

4

What Role for the Minimum Wage in the New Polish Labour Market?

Krzysztof Hagemejer*

1. Role and Functions of the Minimum Wage

Changes in the Polish economy since 1990 have included modifications to minimum wage fixing and reassessments of the economic and social functions of minimum wage rates. The modifications reflect radical changes in the Polish labour market, from excess demand for labour and labour hoarding in state enterprises, to excess supply of labour and growing unemployment. The economic situation has also been characterised by a high, though slowly declining inflation rate and a rapidly emerging private sector.

1.1 An Instrument to Control Wages

Before 1989, the minimum wage had various, parallel functions. It was the basis for wage and salary scales in state enterprises and institutions; the calculation of many other components of workers' remuneration; and the adjustment of minimum amounts for many social benefits (minimum pensions, etc.).

Every adjustment of the minimum wage raised not only general wage levels but also social expenditure. As in all centrally planned economies, in the Polish economy, there was a need to control wages due to soft budget constraints in state enterprises and price controls. Minimum wage fixing was used as one instrument of wage control. That is why, during the 1960s and 1970s, the minimum wage rate was kept at a rather low level and rarely adjusted.

In the 1980s, minimum wage fixing had a special role. With growing inflation, there was a need to introduce some form of indexation mechanism. In the early 1980s, various minimum levels of social benefits were tied to the minimum wage, on the assumption that the minimum wage would be adjusted to keep pace with the cost of living. Later, however, during and after the period of martial law, changes to the minimum wage formula were introduced in order to lower the base for minimum social benefits and to match social expenditure with state budget objectives. Consequently, the minimum wage rate remained unchanged for some years.

* ILO, Social Security Department, Geneva.

During this period, there was another reason for keeping the minimum wage at a low level and for narrowing its definition as much as possible. Different forms of wage control imposed by central government, and state enterprises' attempts to evade it, caused a gradual degeneration of the pay system. The share of controlled basic wages in employees' total remuneration fell to a low level, and was increasingly replaced by various bonuses, allowances, grants and fringe benefits.

After 1982, as part of an economic reform package, state enterprises were allowed to construct their own 'wage systems' according to certain regulations. These regulations included a clause—to raise the share of basic wage rates in total remuneration—requiring that most components of total remuneration,[1] excluding basic wages, be calculated as a percentage of a minimum wage rate and not as a percentage of a personal wage rate on the salary scale, as before. However, as a result of this regulation, average wages in the economy became even more sensitive to minimum wage changes. That was another reason for the official reluctance to change minimum wages; they remained constant between 1982 and 1987.

Amazingly, there were in fact two minimum wage levels during this period: a lower minimum wage that functioned both as a minimum basic wage rate for salary scales in all enterprises that had not introduced wage systems following new regulations, and as a basis for calculating components of other forms of remuneration and social benefits; and a higher minimum wage that was applied only to enterprises introducing new 'wage systems'.[2]

Because the system of fixing minimum wages was used for years to restrain wage and social benefit increases, the official minimum wage rate became disconnected from the average wage, the cost of living and even the lowest wages actually paid. By the end of the 1980s, the number of workers with wages close to the official minimum wage had fallen to insignificant levels. In many enterprises the lowest grades of salary scales simply fell into disuse.

The situation began to change with the political, economic and social upheavals in the direction of a market economy and democracy, although these changes were slow in coming.

1.2 An Instrument to Protect Workers from Poverty

New legislation on minimum wages was introduced in 1990. According to the Labour Code, the minimum wage rate is set by the Ministry of Labour and Social Policy after negotiations with trade union federations. Amazingly, there is no obligation to consult employers' organisations on the

---

[1] It applied to all remuneration components which were presumed not to have a strong motivational impact and treated rather as social benefits.

[2] For a detailed study of minimum wage fixing within the context of wage policies in Poland before 1990 see: Zofia Jacukowicz: 'Płaca minimalna w Polsce i w innych krajach o gospodarce rynkowej,' Instytut Pracy i Spraw Socjalnych, *Studia i Materiały*, z. 10 (371), Warsaw, 1992.

minimum wage rate. This is not only the heritage of the centrally owned and controlled economy of the previous regime but also a symptom of the low level of minimum wages: even for private employers minimum wages do not form an important constraint. This will certainly change in the near future: with the minimum wage progressively increasing employers' organisations will demand the right to participate in minimum wage fixing.

The definition of the minimum wage has also changed. From May 1977 until August 1990, the minimum wage was defined as 'a minimum basic wage rate' for the salary scale. In September 1990, the minimum wage was redefined as 'minimum total remuneration for full–time employment'. This covers the basic wage or salary and other wage or salary components, including fringe benefits. Excluded are:

– bonuses paid out of profits;

– rewards paid from a special 'reward fund';

– allowances paid for long service and on retirement;

– overtime.

Since 1991, when the minimum social benefit level was disconnected from the minimum wage, a general formula has been in use for minimum wage setting, accepted by the Government and trade union federations. The base for the formula is a basket of basic items and services for a single person, in low–income families (first quintile), as reported in household budget surveys conducted by the Central Statistical Office. These basic items and services include food, rent, basic utilities, clothing, health care and public transport. The minimum wage should cover these basic items, taking into account the number of persons in an average low–income family with a single wage–earner and assuming that his wage or salary constitutes 50% of the total income of his family. The minimum wage is recalculated on a quarterly basis, according to an accepted formula based on actual and anticipated changes in the consumer price index.

The idea behind the trade union concept of minimum wage fixing is the 'family wage'. The problem is that the minimum wage earner under the formula is not necessarily part of a low–income family (table 4.1). On the one hand, the trade unions have exerted growing pressure for an increase in the minimum wage level. On the other hand, state enterprises often do not have enough money to pay wages even at the minimum level. Due to social insurance contributions, average labour costs are much higher than the minimum wage itself, and in some enterprises, wages have been well below the minimum level. Although this is plainly against the law, most employees have accepted it.

Table 4.1 *Household Wage Distribution (by Income Percentile Groups), Poland, 1992*

Wage brackets (ZL '000)	Household Income Percentile Groups†					
	Quintile					
	1	2	3	4	5	Total
Below or at the national minimum wage level*	1.89	0.97	0.13	0.11	0.00	0.42
700-800	1.89	0.97	0.65	0.00	0.00	0.49
800-1000	6.09	3.72	1.69	1.09	0.24	1.93
1000-1200	17.02	6.96	4.68	3.04	0.87	4.92
1200–1400	17.02	14.24	7.14	5.00	1.98	7.29
1400–1600	20.59	18.77	10.39	7.07	3.73	10.04
1600–1800	14.08	16.67	14.94	12.72	7.69	12.34
1800–2000	9.24	9.87	17.66	11.63	9.67	11.62
2000–2500	10.08	17.96	25.19	27.17	23.24	22.15
2500–3000	2.10	7.61	9.74	17.28	19.43	13.25
3000–4000	0.00	1.94	6.62	12.28	19.27	10.36
4000 or more	0.00	0.32	1.17	2.61	13.88	5.19
Total	100.00	100.00	100.00	100.00	100.00	100.00

* At the time of this survey (4th quarter, 1991), the minimum wage was ZL 668,000.
† In different income groups the first quintile represents the lowest income group.
Source: B. Gorecki and K. Hagemejer, *Low Income Households*, Warsaw University, mimeo, 1992.

2. Size and Growth of the Minimum Wage

Since 1989, the Polish labour market has been in a state of turbulence. In late 1989, as a result of food price liberalisation, high inflation arrived, with accompanying wage indexation. At the beginning of 1990, a stabilisation plan was implemented; the new policy not only eliminated wage indexation but also introduced wage controls in the form of a tax–based incomes policy (the so–called excess wage growth tax, 'popiwek').[3]

During the first few months of the stabilisation policy, real wages declined by nearly 30%. They recovered slightly during the second half of 1990, but through 1991 and until June 1992 they fell again. There was a slow recovery in real wages observed in the second half of 1992, but in the first three quarters of 1993 they fell again. On average, in the third quarter of 1993, real wages were still more than 15% lower than in 1988 (figure 4.1).

---

[3] For a discussion of income policies in Poland during the early transition period, see F. Coricelli and A. Revenga: 'Wage Policy during the Transition to a Market Economy, Poland 1990–91', World Bank Discussion Paper No. 158, Washington DC, 1992.

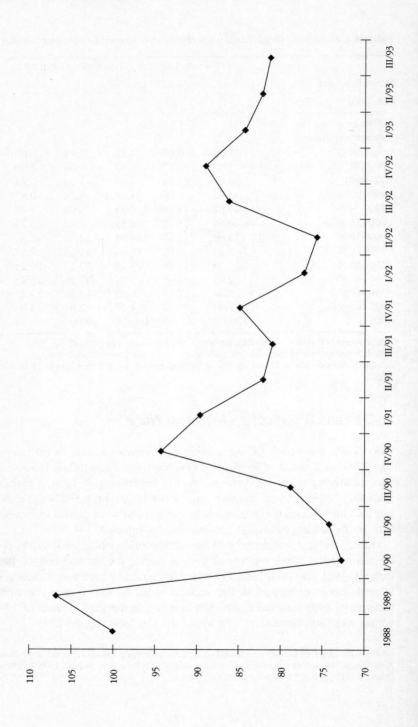

Figure 4.1 *Index of Real Wages, Poland, 1988–93 (1988=100)*

Although in 1993, wage control was still in place, it had lost much of its significance. More powerful mechanisms had displaced it, in particular much harder financial constraints within the state sector. The general situation in the labour market, with an unemployment rate exceeding 15%, also helped limit wage increases.

New legislation on minimum wages introduced in 1990, together with changes in the labour market, enabled the minimum wage rate to rise in relation to average wage levels, and to have a greater role as an effective constraint on micro–economic decisions taken by employees and employers.

Table 4.2 presents minimum wage levels in the 1980s and 1990s compared with the average wage. The minimum wage rose in relation to the average wage after 1990. It was 30% of the average wage at the end of 1990 and about 40% in the middle of 1993. This trend is different from most other Central and Eastern European countries where the ratio decreased over the period. The difference is due to various factors. First, the initial ratio of the minimum wage to the average wage at the end of the

Table 4.2 *The Minimum Wage Compared to the Average Wage, Poland, 1981–93 (ZL '000—figures from 1981 to 1989 are annual averages)*

Year	Average wage*	Minimum wage*	Minimum wage as percentage of average wage
1981	8.3	2.4	28.9
1982	11.5	4.0	34.7
1987	28.5	7.0	24.6
1988	53.1	9.0	16.9
1989	207.0	23.9	11.6
1990 – I	731.0	120.0	16.4
1990 – II	913.0	120.0	13.2
1990 – III	1063.0	203.0	19.1
1990 – IV†	1460.0	440.0	30.1
1991 – I	1657.0	550.0	33.2
1991 – II	1699.0	605.0	35.6
1991 – III	1781.0	632.0	35.5
1991 – IV	2045.0	668.0	32.7
1992 – I	2456.0	875.0	35.6
1992 – II	2650.0	958.0	36.2
1992 – III	3090.0	1167.0	37.8
1992 – IV	3518.0	1350.0	38.4
1993 – I	3653.0	1500.0	41.1
1993 – II	3813.0	1500.0	39.3
1993 – III	4000.0	1650.0	41.3

* Until 1991 net, since 1992 gross (before tax).
† Until September 1990, the minimum wage covered only basic wage rates; since then it has covered all wage/salary components.

1980s was much higher in other countries. For example, in Bulgaria and in the former Czechoslovakia the minimum wage was 50% of the average wage, and it was close to 65% in Romania. Although these countries experienced a downward trend later, the ratio did not fall below 40%, the only exception being Hungary, where it fell to 33%. The situation is somewhat different in Russia and other former Soviet republics, where initial levels were lower than in Poland and have fallen even further since 1989.

The second factor is the disconnection of minimum social benefit levels from the minimum wage, which made government negotiators more eager to accept trade union demands to raise minimum wages. Besides, the Polish trade union federations seem to be more powerful than others in the region. They also have longer experience in free collective bargaining. The absence of employers' representatives in minimum wage negotiations is also significant, although employers in all countries of the region—even when formally present in tripartite negotiations—still seem to be in a weak position.

3. The Minimum Wage and Purchasing Power

The rise in the ratio of the minimum to the average wage does not necessarily mean that the purchasing power of the minimum wage has risen, especially when the fall in real wages has been as dramatic as in Poland. To test this, the minimum wage rate must be related to the cost of living index or to some kind of poverty line. Due to the changes in the definition of the minimum wage, it is not possible to evaluate changes in its real purchasing power between 1989 and 1993. It is possible however to say something about the last quarter of 1990, when the minimum wage definition became stable.

In Poland, a so–called 'social minimum' is calculated quarterly as the value of a basket of basic goods and services. It is not used officially as a 'poverty line' and it has been criticised heavily both by the Government (emphasising its generosity and some methodological deficiencies) and the trade unions (arguing that it is below subsistence level). Nevertheless, it is calculated on a regular basis, thereby making it possible to compare minimum wage rates with some measure of a 'social minimum'.

As the 'social minimum basket' is adjusted quarterly according to the cost of living changes, it is possible to estimate the purchasing power of the minimum wage. However, such a comparison does not allow any conclusions concerning the relation of the minimum wage rate to subsistence.

Table 4.3 compares minimum wage rates (recalculated as 'after tax' since 1992) to the 'social minimum' for a single–person household and for a four–person household (2 adults and 2 children). After the last quarter of

Table 4.3 *Minimum Wage Compared to the Social Minimum, Poland, 1981–93 (ZL '000; figures from 1981 to 1989 are annual averages)*

Year or quarter	Social minimum		Minimum wage (after tax)	Minimum wage as % of soc. min. (1–person household)
	1–person household	4–person household*		
1981	3.2	2.7	2.4	75.0
1982	6.4	5.4	4.0	62.5
1987	14.2	11.8	7.0	49.3
1988	22.5	18.2	9.0	40.0
1989	73.1	60.1	23.9	32.7
1990 – I	413.3	324.2	120.0	29.0
1990 – II	473.9	377.4	120.0	25.3
1990 – III	549.5	437.4	203.0	36.9
1990 – IV†	608.2	487.2	440.0	72.4
1991 – I	737.4	589.1	550.0	74.6
1991 – II	866.4	687.1	605.0	69.8
1991 – III	940.2	746.0	632.0	67.2
1991 – IV	1033.2	812.4	668.0	64.7
1992 – I	1157.0	908.0	804.4	69.5
1992 – II	1317.0	1048.5	871.1	66.1
1992 – III	1505.5	1200.5	1037.7	68.9
1992 – IV	1657.0	1312.5	1184.4	71.5
1993 – I	1812.5	1439.0	1304.4	72.0
1993 – II	2008.0	1596.0	1304.4	65.0
1993 – III	2118.0	1684.0	1424.4	67.3

* Per person.
† Until September 1990 the minimum wage covered only basic wage rates; it now covers all wage/salary components.
Source: Own calculations based on data collected by E. Dabrowska, Economic Department, Ministry of Labour and Social Policy, Warsaw.

1990, measured by the value of the 'social minimum basket', the minimum wage seems to have fluctuated within the range of 65–75% of the social minimum calculated for a single person household. These are fluctuations in its purchasing power, not necessarily reflecting any relation to the subsistence level.

4. Wages, Social Benefits and Total Incomes

In 1990, when real wages and incomes were at their lowest, the minimum wage did not yet play an effective role. Real incomes in wage and salary earners' households dropped by 25%; the share of earned income in total income had fallen in 1989 to 81.5% and in 1990, the share was 82.1%, compared with nearly 85% in 1987. The share of social benefits was 13.9% in 1989 and 13.5% in 1990, compared with 11.4% in 1987. In 1989 and 1990, price increases were greatest for food and energy. Consequently, the food share of total expenditure in wage and salary earners' households rose from 38.7% in 1988 to 44% in 1989 and 46.5% in 1990. In low–income households, the share was 55.9%.

In 1991, average real incomes of wage and salary earners' households stabilised, and there was even a tiny rise of 1.7%. The share of earned income dropped to 80.1%, while the social benefit share increased to 15.9%. In low–income households (1st quintile), the share of earned income in 1990 and 1991 was 73.7% and 69.6% respectively, while the share of social benefit income was 23% and 27.3%. After 1990 food prices stabilised, while rents, fuel, energy, heating, etc. were rising. The percentage of food expenditure in total expenditure decreased to 40.6% in 1991 and to 51.9% in low–income households. The share of basic housing expenditure started to rise. Basic housing expenditure in low–income households amounted to 16% in 1990, 22.5% in 1991 and 15.9% in an average–income household in 1991.

In 1992, real household incomes dropped again by 3%, with the earned income share increasing slightly at the cost of a lower social benefit share. Trends in expenditure patterns were similar to those in 1991.[4] The number of households with relatively low incomes grew. According to some estimates, the percentage of people living below the 'social minimum' was 20% in 1990, 25% in 1991, and 39% in 1992.

5. Wage Differentials

The decline in real wages was accompanied by changes in wage distribution. Table 4.4 presents the main characteristics of wage distribution between 1987 and 1992. Despite the profound changes that have taken place in the economy since 1990, wage differentials have remained moderate. Perhaps one reason for this surprising phenomenon is the unreliability of the data: it is well known that private sector wages are seriously underestimated.

Major changes have taken place among non–manual workers and outside the public sector. Although manual workers' real wages declined the most, the distribution of these wages has not changed much. Some measurements show that wage distribution among state sector manual workers is even more

---

[4] Central Statistical Office: *Metody pomiaru ubostwa*, 1993. The data cover all households including pensioners, farmers and dual occupation workers, where the incidence of poverty is greater than in wage and salary earners' households.

Table 4.4 *Characteristics of Wage Distribution, Poland, 1987–92 (1987–88: public sector only; 1991–92: public and private sectors)*

	Employees	1987	1988	1991	1992	1992 public	1992 private
Maximal equalisation	all	16.4	15.2	17.2	17.7	16.9	20.7
percentage (1)	manual	17.0	15.6	16.5	16.6	16.3	17.5
Concentration	all	0.230	0.213	0.242	0.247	0.236	0.288
coefficient (Lorenz)	manual	0.239	0.219	0.231	0.230	0.255	0.243
Decile ratio (2)	all	275.6	260.5	285.9	292.0	280.2	338.2
	manual	290.4	270.9	284.8	283.1	277.8	300.1
Quartile ratio (3)	all	166.6	162.3	168.1	171.4	168.2	186.6
	manual	170.7	165.0	169.5	170.5	168.9	178.2
Dispersion coefficients (4):							
1st decile based	all	61.3	62.7	61.6	61.6	63.2	57.5
	manual	59.5	60.8	60.7	62.5	63.6	58.9
1st quartile based	all	77.7	78.7	77.9	77.3	78.1	73.9
	manual	76.5	77.6	77.0	77.5	78.2	74.7
3rd quartile based	all	129.5	27.7	130.9	132.4	131.4	138.0
	manual	130.6	128.0	130.4	132.2	132.1	133.1
9th decile based	all	168.8	163.3	179.8	179.8	177.0	194.3
	manual	172.7	164.6	176.9	176.9	176.8	176.9
Coefficient of	all	45.0	40.9	51.9	53.1	49.0	68.0
variation (5)	manual	46.4	41.3	44.0	44.0	42.8	48.4
Hungarian inequality measurements for wages*:							
lower than average (6)	all	1.366	1.341	1.376	1.387	1.368	1.460
	manual	1.385	1.355	1.374	1.370	1.360	1.402
higher than average (7)	all	1.408	1.367	1.453	1.470	1.455	1.588
	manual	1.424	1.372	1.408	1.419	1.431	1.437
overall distribution (8)	all	1.924	1.833	1.999	2.038	1.976	2.318
	manual	1.972	1.859	1.935	1.944	1.922	2.015
Asymmetry index (9)	all	2.021	1.636	4.495	4.056	3.352	4.979
	manual	1.765	1.440	1.660	1.731	1.529	2.485

(1) Percentage of total wage fund in excess of equal wage fund distribution.
(2) Ratio of 9th decile to 1st decile.
(3) Ratio of 3rd quartile to 1st quartile.
(4) Ratio of respective decile or quartile to median.
(5) Ratio of standard deviation to average wage.
(6) Ratio of average wage to average of wages lower than average (AVG/AVGL).
(7) Ratio of average of wages higher than average to average wage (AVGH/AVG).
(8) Ratio of average of wages higher than average to average of wages lower than average (AVGH/AVGL).
(9) Ratio of third order moment to the third power of standard deviation.
* (With AVG=Average wage; AVGL=Average of wages lower than AVG; AVGH=Average of wages higher than AVG.)
Source: Central Statistical Office surveys of employment and wages: 'Zatrudnienie w gospodarce uspolecznionej wedlug wysokossci wynagrodzenia za wrzesien 1988 r', GUS, Warsaw, 1989 (1987–88 data); 'Zadrutnienie w gospodarce narodowej wedlug wysokosci wynagrodzenia za wrzesien 1992 r' GUS, Warsaw 1933 (1991–92 data).

Table 4.5 *Percentage of Workers Receiving Monthly Wages Lower than 50% of the Modal Wage, the Median Wage and the Average Wage, Poland, 1991–92*

	50% of Modal wage		50% of Median wage		50% of Average wage	
	1991	1992	1991	1992	1991	1992
All workers	1.8	0.6	3.3	3.1	6.4	6.7
Manual	2.5	0.8	4.6	4.2	8.6	8.9
Non-manual	0.7	0.3	1.4	1.3	3.3	3.1
Women	2.4	0.6	4.5	4.1	9.1	9.1
Manual	4.6	1.1	8.6	7.6	16.4	16.5
Non-manual	0.8	0.3	1.6	1.5	3.9	3.7
Men	1.3	0.6	2.2	2.2	3.9	4.7
Manual	1.5	0.6	2.5	2.6	4.6	5.5
Non-manual	0.7	0.3	1.1	1.0	2.0	2.0
Private sector	3.7	1.3	6.1	6.8	10.3	12.8
Manual	4.8	1.6	7.9	8.5	13.1	15.6
Non-manual	1.6	0.7	2.8	3.5	5.2	7.3
Women	4.4	1.4	7.5	9.1	13.1	17.4
Men	3.0	1.3	4.6	4.7	7.4	8.6
Public sector	1.4	0.4	2.7	2.2	5.5	5.2
Manual	1.9	0.5	3.8	3.0	7.4	7.1
Non-manual	0.6	0.2	1.1	0.9	2.9	2.3
Women	1.9	0.4	3.8	2.7	8.2	6.9
Men	0.9	0.4	1.6	1.7	3.2	3.8

Source: Central Statistical Office (GUS) surveys on wages and employment; September 1991 and September 1992.

equal now than in the past. This can be explained in part as a result of trade union pressure to secure minimum wage levels. First, there was a notable increase in the ratio of minimum wage to average wage, and second, the tax–based incomes policy was designed in such a way that in state enterprises the cost of raising low wages was much lower than the cost of raising higher wages.

Table 4.5 shows the percentage of workers receiving monthly wages lower than 50% of the modal wage, 50% of the median wage and 50% of the average wage. Whatever we define as the low–wage level, in the public sector the percentage of workers receiving low wages has not changed dramatically. For example, the percentage of workers receiving wages lower than 50% of the average wage was 6.7% in 1992, compared with 7.3% in 1980, 5.3% in 1985, and 4.7% in 1988.

As expected, low wages are much more common among manual workers than among non–manual workers and more common among women than among men. They are also more common in the private sector (figures 4.2, 4.3 and 4.4).

The modal wage was ZL 1,422,000 in 1991 and ZL 2,365,000 in 1992. The median wage was ZL 1,581,000 in 1991 and ZL 2,571,000 in 1992. The

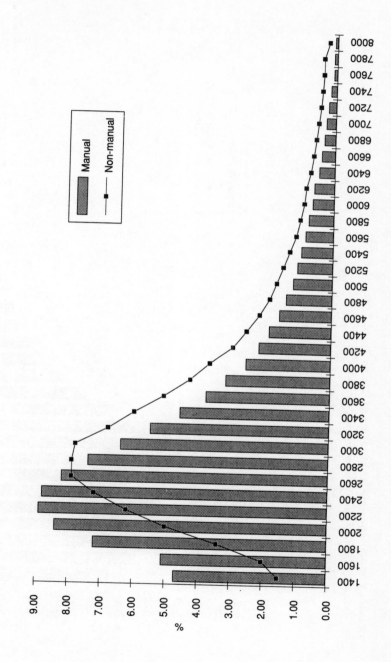

Figure 4.2 *Wage Distribution of Manual and Non-manual Employees, Poland, September 1992 (ZL '000—1,350,000 ZL was the minimum wage in late 1992)*

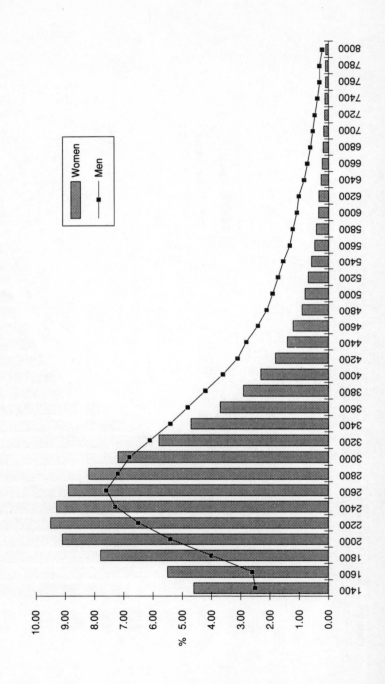

Figure 4.3 *Wage Distribution Among Men and Women, Poland, September 1992*
(ZL '000; ZL 1,350,000 was the minimum wage in late 1992)

Figure 4.4 *Wage Distribution in the Private and Public Sectors, Poland, September 1992 (ZL '000)*

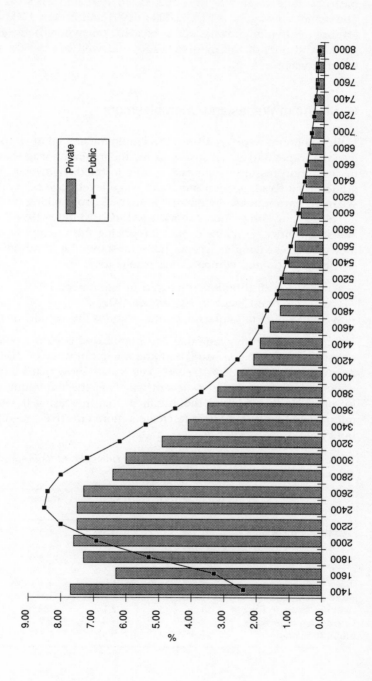

mean average wage was ZL 1,762,000 in 1991 and ZL 3,132,000 in 1992. The minimum wage was ZL 632,000 in 1991 and ZL 1,300,000 in 1992. The level of the minimum wage rate is located somewhere between 50% of the modal and 50% of the median wage, and well below 50% of the mean average wage.

6. Minimum Wages and Unemployment

Is the minimum wage an obstacle to employment? Taking into account low average wages and actual cost of living, the minimum wage seems low, and trade union pressure to increase it fully justified. However, some people argue that a fixed, general minimum wage level, together with high social security contributions, discourages employers from taking on new workers.

The Labour Force Survey, conducted in November 1992 by the Central Statistical Office, contains a question asking the unemployed what wage they would be willing to accept. Table 4.6 shows the distribution of answers to this question and compares the results to:

– actual wage distribution, surveyed in September 1992;
– actual minimum wage in November 1992;
– average actual monthly wage and salary in the second quarter of 1992.

The average monthly wage that an unemployed person would accept was about ZL 1,900,000 compared with the minimum wage of ZL 1,350,000 and the average wage of ZL 3,100,000. The results show that a large number of unemployed were eager to accept wages at the minimum level or even lower. This may support the argument that increasing flexibility in minimum wage fixing could help to create a more effective anti–unemployment policy.

Table 4.6 *Minimum Reservation Wage of the Unemployed, Poland, November 1992 (ZL million unless otherwise stated)*

	All unemployed	Men	Women	Actual wage distribution
Less than 1 million	1.1%	0.8%	1.3%	0.0%
1-1.5 million	36.8%	28.1%	45.1%	4.5%
1.5-2 "	38.3%	37.2%	39.3%	14.1%
2-2.5 "	11.6%	15.3%	8.1%	19.9%
2.5-3 "	8.5%	12.9%	4.4%	17.2%
More than 3 million	3.7%	5.7%	1.8%	44.3%
Average expected wage	1.9	2.1	1.8	
Current average wage	3.1	3.4	2.7	
Minimum wage	1.35	1.35	1.35	

7. Conclusion

This short review of wage developments in Poland during the first years of economic and social transition cannot cover all the relevant issues, nor is it detailed enough to give the full picture of ongoing profound change. However, it shows that Poland, like many other countries in Central and Eastern Europe, is still in the process of adjustment and reformulation of its labour market and social policies to rapid changes in its economic environment. These policies, including minimum wage fixing mechanisms, are still the subject of discussions: among economists, politicians, and the social partners. There are economists who argue that, in transitional economies, one way to ensure sufficient labour market flexibility and to halt rapidly growing unemployment is to abandon or reduce 'unnecessary' labour regulations, including minimum wage regulations, as well as social protection levels to render people more willing to accept work. But there are others who think that in 20th century Europe it is not justified to abandon widely accepted labour standards and norms and to try to return to a 19th century laissez–faire model. Other micro– and macroeconomic policies are available to fight unemployment.

The minimum wage is beginning to be a binding constraint on employers' and employees' decisions. Up until now its level has been too low to play such a role and there were many other constraints on wages imposed by the state. Now, when these constraints (including a punitive tax on wage increases) are to be phased out, space is opening up for more flexible wage setting and wage bargaining. Wage differentials, although increasing, are still small compared with advanced market economies.[5] They will inevitably develop with private sector growth and with overall growth of the economy. High unemployment, especially in certain regions of the country, may depress wages: some limits should be put on this. Minimum wage fixing should take place in accordance with international standards and on the basis of tripartite agreements. Within the framework of these agreements it should be decided what the national minimum wage rate should be, taking into account living costs on the one hand, and the labour market situation, with its great regional differences, on the other.

[5] See D. Marsden (ed.): *Pay and Employment in the New Europe* (Edward Elgar, 1992).

Appendix: Data Sources and their Reliability

Quarterly average wages, real wage changes. Data on wages and employment cover enterprises with five or more employees, and until 1990, only the public sector was included. For measurement of real wage changes, the consumer price index was used. Consumer price index data in Poland are relatively reliable compared with other countries of the region (*Statistical Bulletin*, 7/1993, GUS, Warsaw 1993).

Wage distribution. Representative surveys on wages and employment are carried out each September by the Central Statistical Office. Only full—time employees are surveyed. The private sector was included in the 1991 and 1992 surveys, but wage levels in the private sector are probably considerably underestimated. It is common, within the private sector, to report wages at the minimum level in order to pay minimum social contributions (*Zatrudnienie i wynagrodzenia w gospodarce uspo lecznionej za wrzesien 1988,* GUS, Warsaw 1989; *Zatrudnienie i wynagrodzenia w gospodarce narodowej za wrzesien 1992,* GUS, Warsaw 1993).

Household incomes. Data on wages within household income quintile groups are based on surveys of household incomes and expenditure conducted by the Central Statistical Office.

Minimum wages. Data are from the Ministry of Labour and Social Policy, which is responsible for minimum wage fixing and for negotiations with trade unions.

Unemployment and the wage expectations of the unemployed. There are two sources of data on the unemployed: unemployment registers and the quarterly Labour Force Survey. Both sources show nearly the same total number of unemployed and the same unemployment rates. But this seems to be a coincidence: one–quarter of registered unemployed persons are not unemployed according to the Labour Force Survey (and the ILO's definition of unemployment). On the other hand, one–quarter of those who are unemployed according to the Labour Force Survey are not registered as unemployed in the employment offices, although they are jobseekers. Data on the wage expectations of the unemployed are taken from the Labour Force Survey conducted in November 1992, (*Aktywnosc ekonomiczna ludnosci Polski, Listopad 1992,* GUS, Warsaw 1993).

5

The Impact of the Minimum Wage on Hungarian Wages and Industrial Relations

Jenő Koltay*

1. Introduction

The guaranteed minimum wage in its present form was introduced in 1989. At the end of 1988 the macro level tripartite institution, created by the last government of the 'ancien régime' (as the National Council for the Reconciliation of Interests—OÉT—renamed the Council for the Reconciliation of Interests—ÉT—in 1990 by the new government) was given the right to negotiate and fix an economy–wide, uniform, statutory minimum wage. The amount agreed here is a monthly or hourly basic wage or salary for full–time employment, and is announced in a government decree.

Before 1989 there was no regular minimum wage fixing and it was quite rare when the government increased the minimum wage by a unilateral decision, wage determination being left to central wage regulation—a scheme comparable to Western TIP (tax–based incomes policy) models where wage fund increases exceeding centrally established limits are heavily taxed by the state—and political coordination, complemented by informal plant–level bargaining.

From the beginnings of the command economy until the 1968 economic reforms, the minimum wage as a separate entity was unknown. All wages were determined on the basis of central planning, using such direct tools as administrative control and employer–level targets; more sophisticated wage regulation was deemed unnecessary.

In the immediate postwar period, up to 1949, the minimum wage was established within the framework of a system in which wages were

* Institute of Economics, Hungarian Academy of Sciences, Budapest. This paper was prepared in collaboration with ILO-CEET, Budapest. I am grateful to Daniel Vaughan–Whitehead (ILO-CEET) for his comments and suggestions, as well as to Zsuzsa Orolin (MKI – Labour Research Institute) for her help in collecting and elaborating data and information, István Ónodi Szabó (OMMF-Hungarian Labour Inspectorate) for providing data, and Jean–Jacques Silvestre (LEST-CNRS, Aix-en-Provence) for his comments on my presentation at an international conference on 'The Economic Analysis of Low Pay and the Effects of Minimum Wages' (Arles, 30 Sept.–1 Oct. 1993). Financial support from the European ACE programme and from the Hungarian OKTK (National Social Science Research Programme) is gratefully acknowledged.

determined by collective bargaining, collective agreements being concluded throughout the economy.

2. Wage Control and Minimum Wage Fixing

Freedom of wage determination by the decision of individual employers or by collective agreements at different levels was constrained until recently by central wage control. Evolving from administrative control to parametric regulation or guidelines put a more or less strict upper limit on wage increases without setting a lower limit by fixing a statutory minimum wage and/or by negotiating wage increase minima.

The inherent logic of command economies not only needed—far more than market economies—but also made possible wage control for the purpose of avoiding 'excessive' wage increases, so ensuring the balance of supply and demand in an economy with a generalised shortage of commodities and labour. In these circumstances, with low inflation, no open unemployment, poverty and deprivation not officially admitted, and subsistence minimum calculations kept secret but with wide–ranging paternalist social protection, the case for a regularly adjusted guaranteed minimum wage was weak.

In the reformed version of the command economy, at least in Hungary after 1968, wage control was realised through parametric regulation using a tax levied on enterprise profits (at punitive, progressive rates) in the case of wage increases above predetermined limits (fixed in terms of enterprise wage levels or wage bill). The state control of wage formation, exercised by regulation of wage outflow and of macroeconomic and enterprise–level wage increases, was extended to the formation of relative wages, and enterprise, branch and professional/vocational wage differentials by according preference to individual enterprises from time to time, awarding corrective wage increases to certain industries and professional/vocational categories, and by maintaining a control on the wage hierarchy.

There was a constant struggle and considerable informal bargaining around individual wage policy measures, and the regulation of parameter modifications and concessions. The final outcome in terms of wages paid depended to a large extent on the macroeconomic and political importance of particular enterprises and industries and, within the enterprise, on the bargaining power of core worker groups.

The relatively rare increase in minimum wage levels could be considered as a special kind of central wage policy measure integrated in the above general context of wage determination. It was a sort of non–adjusted or only

Table 5.1 *Wage Determination and Minimum Wage, Hungary, 1945–95*

Year–month	Wage determination		Minimum wage
	General	Minimum	(HUF)
1945	Collective bargaining	Collective bargaining	
1950	Central planning	Central planning	–
1968	Parametric wage control	Government	
1971			960
1976			1 210
1982			1 350
1983			2 000
1988–01	Personal income tax		*3 000
1989–03		Tripartite	*3 700
–10		negotiation (OÉT)	*4 000
1990–02		Tripartite	*4 800
–09		negotiation (ÉT)	†5 600
–11			†5 800
1991–03			†7 000
1992–01	Wage control relaxed		†8 000
1993–02	Wage control abolished		*9 000
1994–02			*10 500
1995–02			*12 200

* Exempt from personal income tax.
† Before personal income tax.
Source: OÉT (National Council for the Reconciliation of Interests), ÉT (Council for the Reconciliation of Interests).

rarely adjusted statutory minimum wage, more a by–product than an instrument of wage control or an important issue in informal wage bargaining.

Between 1971 and 1988 the government 'ordered' the minimum wage on five occasions. This can be interpreted as an adjustment of the lowest wages to average wage growth after a significant time lag. In 1971 the lowest wage actually paid was HUF 960 per month, equal to the declared minimum wage. In 1976, 1982 and 1983 it was somewhat higher than the declared minimum (HUF 1,320, 1,640 and 2,290 as against 1,210, 1,350 and 2,000 respectively). At that time there was no personal income tax (PIT), only a social security contribution, with a strange progressivity, to be paid by employees at all wage levels.

The 1968 economic reform not only implemented wage regulation, it also introduced hierarchically differentiated profit–sharing schemes for all employees according to three occupational categories, without any special measure on wage minima. This liberalisation brought about increasing wage differentials within and among enterprises and branches. Frightened by this, corrective measures reestablishing the status quo were taken as early as 1971–73: regulations modified in favour of asset–intensive large state–owned enterprises, central wage increases to compensate for interbranch wage disparities, and removal of the incentive scheme. Wages and pensions followed the slight (1–2%) inflation and the Government announced a wage minimum of HUF 960 in 1971 which was about 44% of the average wage.

From 1973 wage regulation was combined with wage bill regulation, and in 1975 state–owned enterprises were put under four types of wage control, two in terms of wage level and two in terms of wage bill. The criterion was asset–intensity with the emphasis upon productivity incentives with profits related to wages at the centre. Parallel to these changes the minimum wage was adjusted to HUF 1,210 in 1976, now representing less than 30% of the average wage.

From 1978 individual treatment was more and more demanded by and accorded to large state–owned enterprises, and modifications became more frequent in the regulatory parameters. In 1980 enterprises were regrouped under six basic types of regulation, revised already in 1982. In a more inflationary environment the floor of progressive rates was raised to 9%, then to 12% to allow higher nominal wage increases, followed in 1982 by an increase of the minimum wage to HUF 1,350, remaining around 30% of the average wage.

1983 was an interesting year: on the one hand, wage level regulation was brought back this time rewarding labour saving (staff reducing) enterprises; on the other hand, the minimum wage was for the first time substantially adjusted year on year, to reach HUF 2,000, climbing to 42% of the average wage. This increase was important not only in nominal terms but also regarding purchasing power, although price increases reached even higher levels.

After experimentation with different variants of wage regulation in 1984, in 1985 state–owned enterprises becoming 'self governing' were allowed to choose the appropriate type of new wage regulation linked to wage level, wage increment or government wage determination. The aim was to enhance enterprise autonomy, to encourage responsible behaviour in respect of wages, and to offset bargaining. The minimum wage remained unchanged despite a consumer price inflation above 8% in 1984, down to 5% in 1986 and more than 8% again in 1987.

In 1988, comprehensive tax reform introducing the major taxes of market economies (personal income tax, value added tax, corporate income tax), coupled with a 'technical' increase in before–tax wages, introduced under unfavourable economic circumstances, accelerated price increases and, with nominal wage increases around 30%, gave a cost–push impetus to inflation, almost twice as high as the previous year. In the meantime, the minimum wage was raised by 50% to HUF 3,000 to regain its level against the average wage. The envisaged liberalisation of wages proved to be illusory and regulation became even stricter.

Table 5.2 *Average Wage, Real Wage and Minimum Wage Growth, Hungary, 1971–94*

Year–month (before tax)	Average wage net* (HUF)	(%)	Real wage (%)	Average wage (% of Subsistence minimum)	Minimum wage (% of Average wage)
		(compared to index=100 for previous year)			
1971	2 182a	–	102.3	165	44
1976	4 150b	–	100.1	268	29
1982	4 542	100.0	99.3	236	30
1983	4 761	104.8	96.8	231	42
1984	5 342	112.2	97.6	243	37
1985	5 866	109.3	100.6	245	34
1986	6 291	107.7	101.9	252	32
1987	6 808	108.2	99.4	244	29
1988	7 015	103.0	98.7	220	42
1989–10	8 260	117.7	100.9	220	48
1990–11	10 108	122.3	94.9	180	57
1991–03	11 836	117.4	92.0	150	59
1992–08	13 617	115.0	97.0	124	59
1993–08	16 280c	119.5	–	137	55
1994–04	20 760c	–	–	–	–

* From 1988, after tax wages (gross average wages: 1986 HUF 6,291, 1987 HUF 6,808, 1988 HUF 8,817, 1989 HUF 10,018, 1990 HUF 12,664, 1991 HUF 16,932, 1992 HUF 22,365, 1993 HUF 24,710).
a 1970   b 1980.
c Average of net total earnings (average of gross total earnings 1994–04 HUF 29,322)
Source: Calculations based on Central Statistical Office (CSO), OMK (National Labour Centre) data collected by Zs. Orolin.[2]

In 1989 the enterprises were supposed to pay a standard rate of corporate income tax on the whole amount of wage increments, which were cut back to 14% nominal wage increases, as against a 17% rise in the consumer price index. The minimum wage was raised to HUF 3,700 and later to HUF 4,000 as a guaranteed minimum wage fixed through the OÉT (National Council for the Reconciliation of Interests). The minimum wage amounted to about half the average wage and this minimum wage increase helped to compensate personal income tax which descended to the level of the minimum wage over the next three years.

Wage regulation was still in full force when negotiations started in the National Council for the Reconciliation of Interests (OÉT), which became from the very beginning a forum for macro–level tripartite wage negotiations,

[2] Orolin, Zs.: 'Az 1991. évi minimálbéralku és tanulságai' [The 1991 minimum wage agreement and the lessons learnt from it], *Kereskedelmi Szemle*, No. 3, 1992; 'Minimál–béralku' [The minimum–wage deal], *Figyelő*, 3 December 1992; and 'A minimálbérellenőrzéssel kapcsolatos akcióellenőrzés tapasztalatai' [The experience of the action inspection carried out on minimum–wage control], Országos Munkabiztonsági és Munkaügyi Főfelügyelőség [National Labour Safety and Employment Chief Supervisory Office], 20 June 1994.

taking over progressively the Government's role in wage determination and minimum wage fixing. The OÉT not only fixed minimum wages, but negotiated guidelines for average, minimum and maximum wage increases for enterprises. Government, unions and employers agreed here on enterprise level wage increases free of tax (in enterprises where the wage increase was less than the increase in value added, where the wage bill was less than HUF 20 million, foreign capital participation equal to or more than 20%, and the wage increase less than or equal to 3% in agriculture and the railways).

The first experiences were positive in shifting or at least sharing wage control responsibilities with the emerging social partners. However, increased levies on wages (social security, unemployment, etc.) and a deteriorating financial position imposed tougher constraints on enterprises and moderated their willingness to increase wages. Wage regulation was only partially relaxed and even in 1992 the prohibitive tax could be reactivated if macro–level tripartite wage negotiations had failed to replace it in controlling wage increases in an efficient way. From 1993 onwards, the Government agreed in the Council for the Reconciliation of Interests (ÉT) to remove the tax threat, that is, to abandon central wage control entirely and to rely exclusively on tripartite negotiated guidelines limiting wage increases, without knowing what the future attitude of enterprises toward wage costs and wage increases would be.[3]

As shown above, the case for a guaranteed and regularly adjusted minimum wage became stronger parallel to the loosening, and later the phasing out of wage and price controls. What was formerly a matter of secondary importance is now a primary bargaining issue and an important social protection issue in the light of sharp cost of living rises, a sudden fall in real wages and consumption, and poverty and deprivation accompanying declines in production and employment. Collective bargaining, with the need to set a lower limit to wages and wage increases, first appeared with the guaranteed minimum wage and then with wage guidelines representing not only the maxima but also the minima for negotiated wage increases.

3. Protection of the Low–Paid, Subsistence Minimum Calculation and Minimum Wage Fixing

In an economy where the labour force participation of both men and women was high, the ratio of wage earners in the population being among the highest in the world, an almost exclusive state sector, price and wage

---

[3] Cf. doubts expressed in Köllő, J. (1993): 'Megjegyzés a háromoldalú bérmegállapodások hatásosságáról' ['Note on the effectiveness of tripartite wage agreements'], *Közgazdasági Szemle*, 1993, No. 4.

controls and a compressed wage scale, little or no inflation, no open unemployment and poverty officially nonexistent, there was no felt need for separate protection of the low–paid by minimum wages or other means.

As in other centrally planned economies, the social costs of labour force reproduction were determined for planning purposes, using the 'objective' method of optimum or minimum consumption norms in order to calculate subsistence income levels for different types of family. These excluded such basic items as free education or health care, but included the cost of other items, regardless of whether they were to be paid from the household's own income or financed by the state (enterprise or budget).

For a long time, more or less regular general wage increases—except for shorter periods of stagnation—and benefits in kind fulfilled the role of wage and incomes policy. Changes began towards the end of the 1970s: price controls were loosened, inflation went up and more efforts were made to curb the purchasing power of the population. Restrictive policies managed to cut real wages, showing a decreasing trend from that time onwards, but did not diminish total population income outflow. Transfer payments and social benefits continued to rise, as a result of which the proportion of wage earnings in total incomes fell, especially for low paid groups. Incomes from other sources, outside the scope of the state control machinery, were also on the rise.

Again, policymakers felt no need for a regularly adjusted minimum wage. However, subsistence minimum calculations were maintained and refined in the 1980s, when in some other countries of the region they were neglected. In Hungary, subsistence minimum calculations raised ever greater interest, but it was only in 1985 that subsistence minima figures, calculated by the Central Statistical Office (CSO), were published for the first time in the postwar period. Unpublished figures for 1984 showed a HUF 2,500 subsistence minimum and a HUF 3,050 social minimum per head for working families against a HUF 2,000 minimum wage. Neither politicians nor experts took a position regarding the extent to which the subsistence minimum should be covered by wages and/or social benefits complementing wages.

CSO calculations used a mixed approach: departing from consumption norms for food and housing (except for investment) costs and accounting for the rest in proportion to their weight in total family expenditures.[4]

In the 1960s, research on low incomes and poverty was based on unpublished Central Statistical Office calculations expressing the subsistence minimum as a percentage of average/median incomes and using different

[4] The first are measured quite exactly using nutrition norms and a consumption basket method, the second employing regression analysis to calculate a lumpsum of all other expenditures belonging to a given food expenditure level, taking household incomes and expenditures in their reality.

ratios for social or biological minima. Alternative calculations, based on consumption norms, in 1980 and 1982 were contested both by professionals and politicians, but redone later by a local group of social workers and widely cited in social policy and minimum wage debates.

The subsistence minimum published in 1984 continued to rise, while the minimum wage fixed in 1983 remained unchanged until 1988 so that it decreased in proportion to the subsistence minimum (table 5.3). In 1989 some government decrees used a HUF 4,300 subsistence minimum, while the Central Statistical Office published a HUF 4,470 figure; the minimum wage was increased to HUF 3,700, then to HUF 4,000. The alternative calculation gave a figure of HUF 5,689 for districts of Budapest.

Heated debate and systematic change called for a revision of the Central Statistical Office calculations: the new figures, based on the 1991 household panel survey, are published quarterly. A special subsistence minimum commission, including employees' and employers' representatives, formed in 1989 by the new Parliament, agreed on the primary importance of subsistence minimum calculations in orienting the wage, tax and social security systems. They opted for an objective, but socially determined subsistence minimum with solid theoretical foundations, to be used as a reference point but not subject to bargaining.

It is widely agreed that minimum wage negotiations should take into account the evolution of the subsistence minimum. Macroeconomic and market circumstances allow the subsistence minimum to play such a role in Hungary, where inflation is largely kept under control and there are no shortages coupled with a sharply dichotomous double price system as in certain other countries of the region.

In the last few years, the weight of wage earnings in total incomes has further diminished, particularly the share of wage earnings in the public sector, due to the dramatic falls in manning levels with a shift to unemployment, inactivity or the private sector. The same reasons explain the further rise of transfer payments (unemployment benefits, social assistance payments), capital and other non–wage incomes.

Increasing inequalities in wages, incomes and wealth, signalling poverty and deprivation for those at the bottom of the scale, now present a strong argument for a statutory minimum wage and its regular adjustment to protect the low–paid, either in the shrinking public sector or the expanding private sector. Of course, a low wage does not always mean a low income, and there may be said to be two types of household including minimum wage earners: those less dependent on wages, with substantial non–wage incomes, and those very much wage dependent, with negligible non–wage incomes living often below subsistence minimum level. We do not know much about the relative weight of the two groups, the majority, and probably most family–heading minimum wage earners, are to be found in the second group, although it must be noted that those working in the private sector often report minimum level remuneration for tax purposes while enjoying a considerable income (see below for a trade union–proposed remedy).

The best year for the minimum wage in Hungary was 1990, the year in which across–the–board changes from a monolithic party–state to parliamentary democracy took place; it increased three times in the course of the year, to HUF 4,800, HUF 5,600 and HUF 5,800 and, for the first time, rose above subsistence minimum level. However, it was subsequently adjusted only irregularly, increasing in January 1992 to HUF 8,000, and in February 1993 to HUF 9,000. It then remained unchanged for the rest of 1993, and fell again below the subsistence minimum level. In early 1995 it was fixed at HUF 12,200.

Policymakers, social partners and experts have reached no consensus on how close the minimum wage should follow the subsistence minimum and

Table 5.3 *Subsistence Minimum, Consumer Prices and Minimum Wage, Hungary, 1971–95*

Year–month	Subsistence minimum (HUF per head)*	(%)†	Consumer prices (%)†	Minimum wage (%)†	(% of SM)
1971	1 320	–	102.0	–	72.7
1976	1 550	–	105.0	126.0	78.0
1982	1 920	124.0	106.9	112.0	70.3
1983	2 060	107.0	107.3	148.0	97.0
1984	2 200	107.0	108.3	100.0	90.9
1985 (published)	2 390	109.0	107.0	100.0	83.7
1986	2 500	105.0	105.3	100.0	80.0
1987	2 790	112.0	108.6	100.0	71.7
1988	3 180	114.0	115.7	150.0	94.3
1989 –03	3 760	118.0	–	123.0	98.4
–10	–	–	117.0	133.0	–
1990 –02	–	–	–	120.0	–
–09 (official)	4 990	133.0	–	140.0	112.2
–11	5 600	–	128.9	145.0	103.5
1991 –01	6 450	115.0	–	100.0	89.9
–03	7 848	–	135.0	121.0	89.2
1992 –01	8 870	113.0	–	114.0	90.2
–08	10 980	–	123.0	114.0	72.9
1993 –02	–	–	–	113.0	–
–08	11 830	108.0	122.5	113.0	76.0
1994	–	–	–	107.0	–
1995	–	–	–	116.2	–

* Calculated from Central Statistical Office data, taking the average of different types of household.
† % of previous year.
Source: Calculations based on CSO and National Labour Centre (OMK) data collected by Zs.Orolin.

which subsistence minimum should serve as a reference point: should it equal the subsistence minimum in the case of a single wage earner as advocated by the unions (mainly the old–new MSZOSZ), or should it fill the income gap left by an average wage plus benefits for two children in a two–adult, two–children household, up to the family subsistence minimum level advocated by some experts. The differences are significant: the first amounted in November 1993 to HUF 13,777 for an urban single wage earner and to HUF 9,767 per head for an urban two–adult, two–children family. In September 1994 the respective figures were HUF 19,200 and HUF 13,750.

In any case, not only the link, but also the difference between the minimum wage and the subsistence minimum is evident in the present situation. The second is a social category to be covered at household level partly by wages, partly by other incomes, principally social benefits. Responsibility for the latter shared by employers, government and local government is in the process of redistribution, with a tendency to shift the burden from enterprises to central government and from central government to local government: much confusion reigns around a safety net having to harmonise legitimate demands and scarce resources.

Even if the regular adjustment of the minimum wage to the evolution of the subsistence minimum or to average wages is socially indicated and strongly supported on the employee side, it remains controversial—among other reasons—because of its unclear impact on employment and wages above the minimum level. Employers are already aware of the social implications of minimum wages, but they are also becoming more and more sensitive to the role of the minimum wage in their total wage costs. Given the considerable decline in employment and the low number of vacancies, jobs paid at a not fully adjusted minimum wage level or even below, are more attractive for job seekers than under normal circumstances; although a great deal depends on the level of unemployment benefits (see below).

4. Wage Bargaining and Minimum Wage Bargaining

Hierarchical coordination has already been loosened by ambivalent reforms in wage determination and industrial relations, but only the transition to a market economy, implementing parliamentary democracy and redistributing property rights, opened up the prospect of collective bargaining and social partnership. The relevant legal frameworks are in place, but economic difficulties and asymmetric industrial relations—with a still over–powerful state, weak or still emerging employers and unions—do not bode well at present for collective bargaining between employers and unions.

Negotiations are active at macro level in the tripartite Council for the Reconciliation of Interests (ÉT), but branch and enterprise level collective bargaining remains weak and sporadic. Joint committees (with equal representation on both sides) are still lacking. The employees' side is fragmented, the employers' side even more; the latter does not have a branch organisation structure on the basis of which to negotiate or the authority to make and enforce agreements in the expanding private sector.

In 1992, a good year from this point of view, only 21 branch level collective agreements were concluded (covering only 790,000, that is 40% of employees in industry) on average wage increase minima; these were only recommendations and so meant little to individual employees. At enterprise level about 400 agreements were registered (covering 570,000 employees), containing more concrete, and in some cases binding wage increases.

The Council for the Reconciliation of Interests can be developed into an appropriate institution to negotiate minimum wages and—while still necessary—wage guidelines, but it should not take over the wage determining function of bilateral collective agreements. Government, unions and even employers have found it easier, and cheaper, to agree on minimum wage increases than on overall wage increases or overall wage increase limits.

The social partners consented to minimum wage negotiations taking centre stage in bargaining, but had divergent views on the extent of minimum wage increases. The employers' positions (including the state, still a dominant employer) have been formed under increasing wage cost constraints. No side, however, had crystallised ideas on the role and functions of a guaranteed minimum wage in a transforming economy, but all were eager to demonstrate some short–term positive results from the interminable negotiations. Government and unions badly needed some success to help consolidate their positions in the ever more painful transition process.

From the beginning of tripartite negotiations in the National Council for the Reconciliation of Interests (OÉT), and then in the Council for the Reconciliation of Interests (ÉT), the unions old and new were united in pushing the minimum wage increase before other bargaining issues, the majority of the fragmented union side following the one–dimensional social approach of MSZOSZ in demanding minimum wages in line with or higher than the subsistence minimum calculated by the CSO (HUF 4,000 for 1989, HUF 5,800 for 1990, HUF 8,200 for 1991, and HUF 9,700 for 1992). Only LIGA, on the basis of macroeconomic considerations, was afraid of negative consequences on prices and employment.

The ÉT partners accepted negotiation in terms of the (revised) subsistence minimum, reflecting the continuously deteriorating living conditions, and agreed to important minimum wage increases for 1990 and 1991. These brought the minimum wage in 1990 above the subsistence minimum level only to fall below it again the following year (table 5.3). There was more enthusiasm on the government side than on that of the employers', ever more conscious of the direct, indirect and potential impact of minimum wage increases on wage costs, with particular regard to increases in wage related levies, such as unemployment benefits and other social contributions, and the wage hierarchy.

They were told by the Government that what the public sector, as the poorest employer, could afford should be reasonable for all other employers. The seriously divided employers were solid enough on this issue: minimum wage increases should remain in line with the employers' ability to pay in the worst case economic scenario. If not, numerous low–paid jobs would disappear. In compensation for higher wage costs they vainly proposed lower taxes; their next step was to demand (temporary) relief from the minimum wage increase. The agreement reached on this point raised the delicate problem of differentiated minimum wage fixing for agriculture, but also for other branches in which the average wage was close to the minimum wage (see below).

In demanding higher minimum wages the trade unions were also aiming for increases in other wages. This familiar 'abuse' is widespread in Hungary today. Real wages are falling, but the scope for wage increases is rather limited; the social partners should take over the Government's role in wage determination, but the necessary institutions and routines of collective bargaining are lacking. In such circumstances minimum wage negotiations using social arguments serve partly as a substitute for wage bargaining.

The confusion caused by the interregnum in wage determination is reflected in the complementary 'agreement' on economy–wide wage minima at different levels of the wage hierarchy taking the minimum wage as a starting point. The ÉT partners agreed on this in 1992, but could not decide if it represented an obligation or only a proposal.

The general role of the minimum wage as a bargaining tool was reinforced by the new wage scale in the very large public service sector, built directly upon it. To attenuate its budgetary impact the Government suspended this link and separated public sector wage negotiations with the creation of the Public Sector Council for the Reconciliation of Interests (KIÉT). Wage decisions can have opposite effects on the budget: higher wages, even higher minimum wages, because subject to taxation, can increase revenues, and bring additional savings in social expenditure.

Since the introduction of personal income tax, trade union demands have centred on after–tax wages, while in the case of the low paid they have fought for a tax exempt minimum wage and subsistence minimum. They succeeded in regaining the first only in 1993. Employers take a different position in negotiations, focusing not on the net amount received by the worker (after the employee's social security contribution and personal income tax have been deducted), but on total wage costs, even in the case of minimum wages.[5] Needless to say they are in favour of tax reductions, which directly or, in the case of personal income tax, through lowering wage demands, can moderate wage cost increases.

5. Enforcement and Fragmentation of the Minimum Wage

The guaranteed minimum wage was introduced in a period when market economy institutions were being brought into being and the economy was in deep recession. Market losses, falls in production, bankruptcy, and fiscal drag tended to enlarge the scope of the minimum wage and the number of those paid below it (not to mention those paid, sometimes considerably above it but underreporting).

There were already signs at the end of the 1980s that much larger groups than the young and the unskilled were being paid around the minimum wage level. The deepening of the economic crisis widened the pool of enterprises and branches paying low wages, ranging from the long–term disadvantaged to those who had only recently lost their old central wage concessions, including traditional small enterprises, craftsmen, cooperatives, communal services, light industry, agriculture and, increasingly, public services like education and health, and some heavy industry.

According to ÉT (Council for the Reconciliation of Interests) figures, in 1992 for example 27% of all employees (585,000, excluding public service), 52% of those working in agriculture, 41% in light industry, 32% in trade, 22% in food processing, 9% in electrical energy production, and 6% in chemicals were paid below HUF 9,000, the minimum wage negotiated for the following year.[6] A Ministry of Labour survey gives a lower figure, around 300,000 in May 1992 for the total number of those concerned in the minimum wage increase, 24% in agriculture, 16% in light industry, etc.[7]

It was no secret that branches in the worst position lagged years behind the minimum wage increases. Enterprises in difficulties often 'forget' or are unable to pay the guaranteed minimum wage to their workers, just as they do not pay, for example, social security contributions. The rare and approximate figures show that in 1988, 28% of those employed in agriculture, 27% in retail, 15% in crafts, and 13% in light industry earned less than the HUF 3,700 minimum wage.

---

[5] The difference is extremely high by international comparison: 20–44% personal income tax, social security contributions of 10% for employees and 44% for employers, and unemployment insurance contributions of 1.5% for employees and 5% for employers.
[6] *Magyar Hírlap*, 1 December 1992. [7] *Figyelő*, 3 December 1992.

In 1990, about one–quarter of all wage earners were, at least temporarily, below the minimum wage, raised to HUF 5,600 in September: half of them worked in agriculture, the rest in textiles, trade, transport, and construction. Even in public services one–fifth were affected by the minimum wage increase. The wage regulations still valid at that time levied a prohibitive tax on enterprises for all wage increases above a certain limit (then above a 3% increase of the wage bill); the personal income tax levied on minimum wages between 1990 and 1992 should also be mentioned in this context.

Tripartite negotiations in 1989 had already accepted a couple of months' delay in increasing the minimum wage in agriculture and in the non–agricultural cooperative sector. At the end of 1991, when the minimum wage was raised to HUF 7,000, an agreement on the increase was allowed later on. In 1992 textiles and food processing obtained unconditional relief from paying the HUF 8,000 minimum wage.

Gradually, a kind of branch–level minimum wage bargaining has emerged in a significant part of the economy with the approval of the ÉT (Council for the Reconciliation of Interests), including the Government. In the meantime, repeated checks are carried out to enforce the minimum wage increases throughout the economy.

The last economy–wide control campaign in May 1994 surveyed 1,845 employers and 104,033 employees in all sectors, branches and professional categories in proportion to their respective weights (without being statistically representative). The results confirm the tendencies of recent years for the branch and sectoral distribution of underpayment (tables 5.4 and 5.5).

Table 5.4 *Distribution of Underpayment by Branch, Hungary, 1994*

	Number of employers		Number of employees	
	total	involved in underpayment	total	involved in underpayment
Construction	135	24	10 647	143
Industry	550	107	43 259	665
Trade	472	99	11 018	289
Catering	259	96	2 650	262
Transport	69	7	4 040	9
Health and social care	33	3	6 990	10
Agriculture, forestry, fishing	134	30	11 404	105
Post, telecommunications	26	2	4 593	17
Education	39	0	2 409	0
Other	128	31	7 023	115
Total	1 845	399	104 033	1 615

Source: Calculations based on data collected by OMMF (Hungarian Labour Inspectorate), May 1994.

Table 5.5 *Distribution of Underpayment by Sector, Hungary, 1994*

	Number of employers		Number of employees	
	total	involved in underpayment	total	involved in underpayment
State enterprise	50	6	7 253	17
Corporation*	1 124	198	68 747	965
Cooperative	180	48	14 329	213
Public service	86	6	9 659	19
Other	405	141	4 045	401
Total	1 845	399	104 033	1 615

* In private, state or mixed ownership.
Source: Calculations based on data collected by OMMF (Hungarian Labour Inspectorate), May 1994.

Table 5.6 *Distribution of Underpayment by Category, Hungary, 1994*

	Total number of employees	Underpaid employees as proportion of total (%)	Amount of Underpayment (HUF)		
			<1 000	1–2 000	>2 000
			(number of employees concerned)		
Manual	26 085	25.1	904	414	239
Non–manual	77 948	74.9	41	13	4
Unskilled	70 771	68.0	504	239	157
Skilled	33 262	32.0	449	186	80
Women	42 420	40.8	404	170	89
–Under 18	778	0.7	9	6	4
Part–timers	2 281	2.2	63	23	2
Pensioners	2 798	2.7	65	37	42

Source: Calculations based on data collected by OMMF (Hungarian Labour Inspectorate), May 1994.

As shown in table 5.6 the same holds for the categories concerned: manual workers are proportionally 8 times more likely than other groups to be paid below the minimum wage, unskilled workers 2.7 times more than skilled workers, part–time workers 2.5 times more than full timers, working pensioners 3.3 times more than other groups (no conclusions were drawn as regards under 18s, because of their low representation in the sample). The only significant change is the gradual disappearance of gender differences (40.8% of underpaid workers are women; table 5.6): previously women were three times worse off than men in this respect.

Underpayment can reach 20% or more, though in the majority of cases it is around 10%. This gives a period of about a year as the typical delay in honouring minimum wage adjustments in branches and enterprises that are lagging behind.

Typical cases of employers' negligence are revealed again and again: they tend not to follow changes in the minimum wage if they occur within a year of the last changes; they fail to calculate the proper minimum wage of employees working more or less than the standard working time; they pay disproportionately less to part–time workers and do not pay more for extra hours, arguing that they are simply honouring the official minimum wage. If there is no contract or record of the wage actually paid, which happens frequently in small and medium–size enterprises, it may readily be supposed, but it is difficult to prove that underpayment has taken place. The same holds where part of remuneration is paid in the form of individual incentives or profit sharing.

Perhaps the abovementioned fragmentation of the national minimum wage at branch level, together with some hints from the international youth minimum wage debate, gave the idea for a recent trade union (MSZOSZ) proposal on hierarchically differentiated minimum wages. The three–stage structure would add to the present minimum wage another for skilled workers and a third for those with a higher education. The justification for this is twofold: first, it is only fair to reflect a person's skills in his remuneration; second, this would represent an effective measure to combat payment according to qualification level but underreported.

The new MSZOSZ–friendly Government and the employers have so far expressed no opinion, although this proposal is on the bargaining table despite the failure of the negotiations on a global economic and social agreement envisaged by the Government. In the context of the present analysis, this means not only potential further fragmentation, but also the most recent use of the minimum wage as a universal bargaining tool.

6. Conclusion

In most market economies minimum wages have for a long time been fixed as part of the bargaining process, with government intervention to a greater or lesser extent, by legislation or collective agreement. The original and still primary objective is to improve the position of the lowest paid employees, although it has gained a role of increasing importance in the whole wage bargaining process, influencing increases along the wage hierarchy.

With positive growth, controlled inflation and a balanced budget, minimum wages are regularly adjusted and generally observed, and their impact on other wages and wage costs does not compromise macroeconomic policy goals. Minimum wage increases remain in line with average wage growth and the number of workers receiving the minimum wage does not increase or tends to decrease.

In Hungary, an economy moving from central control to free wage bargaining, the bargaining function of the minimum wage may prevail over its social function, becoming more important than ever in the difficult social and economic context. Underdeveloped bargaining institutions and deficient bargaining skills on the one hand, and falls in production and employment, high inflation and a budget deficit on the other make it difficult or impossible to harmonise the social and bargaining functions of the minimum wage.

In circumstances of an overextended wage hierarchy, shrinking average wages in real terms and more workers paid around the minimum level or below, intensifying minimum wage demands and agreed increases can hardly assure effective protection for the low–paid or do much for wages above the minimum.

Bargaining 'abuse' of the minimum wage is now inevitable, but a guaranteed minimum wage remains an appropriate means to protect the low–paid. Of course, it can not assure the subsistence minimum alone, even in an economy where inflation is kept under control and there are no shortages. It should share this task with other benefits financed by enterprises, and central and local government.

For the emerging social partners, especially the weak trade unions and the government, the minimum wage has a particularly legitimate function. An agreement on a minimum wage increase can be a rare achievement, relatively easy to obtain and demonstrating social sensitivity and a willingness to cooperate in difficult times. The high level and the persistence of unemployment, however, raises the difficult question of the impact of minimum wage increases on employment.

6

Have Minimum Wages Hit Employment in the Czech Transformation?

Alena Buchtikova*

1. Minimum Wage Protection in the Czech Republic

The main goal of economic reform in the Czech Republic is the transformation of a centrally planned economy into a market economy. The process of transformation started in 1990 and comprises the following important policies: macroeconomic anti–inflationary policy, restrictive monetary and fiscal policy, privatisation, price liberalisation, foreign trade liberalisation, internal convertibility and social safety–net policy. As economic reform inevitably entails substantial upheaval in the Czech economy, wage policy too must fall in line with it. This aspect is particularly important for an understanding of the process of wage determination in the Czech Republic.

Wage determination is the result of the collective bargaining at all levels of trade unions, employers, and government.[1] It is implemented by a system of laws, collective agreements and government decrees.

The national minimum wage was set for the first time on the basis of tripartite political consensus. As there was no previous experience upon which to draw, the starting level of the minimum wage was based on two assumptions: first, the minimum wage cannot be lower than minimum living costs and, second, it must be higher than 50% of the average wage. The last assumption reflects minimum wage levels in European Union (EU) countries.

As a result of the Tripartite Agreement the national minimum wage was for the first time set in the General Agreement for 1991 at CSK 2,000 monthly or CSK 10.80 for employees on an hourly wage tariff system.[2] This minimum wage was confirmed by *Government Directive No. 99/1991 of 25 February*, for all employees independently of their occupational classification, form of work, and the performance and solvency of their employers.

---

* Czech National Bank.

[1] For more details about the institutional structure of wage bargaining, see A. Buchtikova and V. Flek: 'Wage Determination in Czechoslovakia: Government Power versus Trade Union Power', Czech National Bank, Prague, 1992.

[2] The members of the Czech tripartite body are the Czech Government, the Czech–Moravian Confederation of Trade Unions, consisting of 40 sectoral trade unions with 4 million members, and the employers' associations.

Table 6.1 *Trend in the Real Minimum Wage and the Real Average Wage, Czech Republic, 1st quarter of 1991–2nd quarter of 1993, (CSK; 1989=100)*

	Minimum wage	Average wage	CLI* wage	Real min. wage	Real aver. wage	Proportion real min.wage/ aver. wage (%)
Aver. 1990	–	3 247	109.9	–	–	–
1991						
1st quarter	2 000	3 324	156.5	1 278	2 124	60.17
2nd quarter	2 000	3 613	168.9	1 184	2 139	55.36
3rd quarter	2 000	3 747	171.8	1 164	2 181	53.38
4th quarter	2 000	4 597	175.2	1 142	2 624	43.51
Aver. 1991	2 000	3 790	168.1	1 190	2 255	52.77
1992						
1st quarter	2 200	4 059	180.3	1 220	2 251	54.20
2nd quarter	2 200	4 607	183.1	1 202	2 516	47.75
3rd quarter	2 200	4 628	188.1	1 170	2 460	47.54
4th quarter	2 200	5 462	197.8	1 112	2 761	40.28
Aver. 1992	2 200	4 677	187.3	1 175	2 497	47.04
1993						
1st quarter	2 200	5 175	219.3	1 003	2 359	42.51
2nd quarter	2 200	5 809	222.9	987	2 606	37.87
3rd quarter	2 200	5 769	227.8	966	2 532	38.13
4th quarter	2 200	6 615	234.6	938	2 820	33.26
Aver. 1993	2 200	5 840	226.2	973	2 582	37.67

* Cost of Living Index.
Source: Own computations, based on the data of the Czech Statistical Office.

In the first quarter of 1991 the level of the national minimum wage represented 60.2% of the level of the average monthly wage. It remained unchanged until the end of 1991, when its proportion of the continuously rising average monthly wage fell to 43.5% (table 6.1).

The minimum wage was adjusted only once to the value of CSK 2,200 or CSK 12 for employees on an hourly wage tariff system by *Government Directive No. 53/1992 on the minimum wage* in January 1992. This minimum wage level was still in operation in late 1993 and represented 54.2% of the 1992 first–quarterly average monthly wage, but only 40.3% of the 1992 fourth–quarterly average monthly wage, 37.9% of the 1993 second–quarterly average monthly wage, and only 33.26% of the 1993 fourth–quarterly average monthly wage (table 6.1 and figure 6.1).

As mentioned above, minimum wage determination is the result of wage bargaining at all levels of industrial relations. The national minimum wage fixed by the Czech Tripartite Body is regarded as a starting point for wage negotiations at the lower levels of wage bargaining. The principles of bargaining in the process of making collective agreements between trade unions

Figure 6.1 *Minimum Wages as a Proportion of Average Wages, Czech Republic, 1st Quarter 1991–2nd Quarter 1993 (%)*

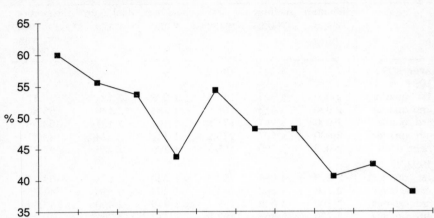

and employers, with the contingent cooperation of the Government, are stated in *Law No. 2/1991 on collective bargaining*.[3] According to this Law the wage claims determined in a collective agreement at enterprise level cannot be lower than those in the higher–type collective agreement.

Substantial changes in the field of wage protection were investigated at the beginning of 1992, when new principles of wage reform were laid down in *Law No. 1/1992 on wages, bonuses for emergency duties, and average earnings*. The aim of this Law is the creation of conditions required for wage policy liberalisation and, in the meantime, to protect wages. According to *Law No. 1/1992*, wages set within individual or collective agreements and average hourly and/or monthly earnings cannot be lower than the level of the minimum wage set by the government directive. Collectively agreed wage rates are therefore higher than both the national minimum wage and those in the higher–type collective agreements.

Sectoral collective agreements are valid for all employees (including non–union members) in enterprises whose owners and trade unions are members of the sectoral association which signed them. In 1993 there were 35 sectoral collective agreements between sectoral trade unions and sectoral employers' associations, but only some included minimum wage settlements. The main part of these agreements involved only recommendations for minimum wage levels or minimum wage tariffs for wage negotiation at enterprise level.

[3] The levels of wage bargaining are the national level, (the Czech Tripartite Body); the sectoral level; and the enterprise level.

Table 6.2 *Average Minimum Wages Negotiated at Enterprise Level, Czech Republic, 1993, (CSK)*

Sector	Number of firms	Minimum wage (CSK/Hour)
Textiles, clothing and fur industry	2	12.75
Restaurants, hotels and tourism	1	12.60
Printing industry	10	12.00
Glass, china and ceramics	18	13.40
Woodworking, forestry and water	39	13.32
Chemicals	26	13.24
Metal processing	38	13.29
Construction	44	13.51
Mining and geological	3	15.10
Medical and social services	1	12.00
Services	4	13.63
Transport and motor vehicle servicing	4	13.50
Agriculture	1	14.00
Food industry	8	13.61

Source: Trexima Labour Cost Information System.

The Ministry of Labour and Social Affairs has the right to extend the validity of some higher–type (sectoral) collective agreements to enterprises in which employers and trade unions are not members of the sectoral associations which signed the agreement.

Table 6.2 shows the average rates of the minimum wages negotiated at enterprise level on the basis of sectoral collective agreements for 1993, the national minimum wage being 12 CSK/hour.

Where a collective agreement does not exist or does not include wage setting, the wage must not be lower than the minimum wage tariff relevant for the given employee. The system of minimum wage tariffs plays an important role in the wage protection of all employees in the Czech Republic, especially in the present period of economic and political trans-formation. There is a large number of new private entrepreneurs with little experience in wage determination, who would be more than willing to impose inadequate remuneration on their employees. Minimum wage tariffs protect all categories of workers: they are also binding on all employ-ers outside collective agreements (or without a wage settlement in such an agreement) with enterprise trade unions.

The whole tariff system is based on the evaluation of qualifications, skills, responsibilities and working conditions and includes 12 tariff rates. After the enactment of *Law No. 1/1992,* the minimum wage tariff rates were set by *Government Directive No. 43/1992 of 23 December 1991 on the setting of minimum wage tariffs and preferential treatment for difficult, unhealthy and night work.* The minimum wage tariff for the first group was set at the level of CSK 2,200 (or CSK 12 for employees on the hourly wage system), that is, at the level of the minimum wage. It was changed by *Government Directive No. 333/1993 of 1 December 1993* to CSK 2,340 (or CSK 12.80 for employees on the hourly wage system).

In accordance with the recommendations of the International Labour Organisation and its *Convention on the Minimum Wage*, the minimum wage tariff for the first tariff rate was not set below but at the level of the national minimum wage.

In general, an employer has two possibilities:

a) He can sign a collective agreement with the trade unions which includes provisions on wage setting. In this case he is not obliged to respect minimum wage tariffs in all categories, only the national minimum wage (12 CSK/hour). Despite the fact that the minimum wage tariff system usually represents the trade unions' minimum wage claims in the process of wage negotiation, an employer can set some wage tariffs below the minimum. The gap created at the end of 1993 between the minimum wage and the first (minimum wage) tariff rate is another reason for employers to adhere to the process of wage bargaining.

b) An employer may opt out of wage bargaining with the trade unions. In this case, he is obliged to honour the minimum wage rates in all tariff categories and he must pay the minimum wage rate (12.80 CSK/hour) for employees in the first tariff group. According to the Czech–Moravian Confederation of Trade Unions the proportion of employees protected by the minimum wage has grown and represented approximately 36% of all employees in 1993.

The minimum wage in the Czech Republic currently has a number of features that are different from those characteristic of a market economy:

– The minimum wage must protect employees' wages and living standards during the period of economic reform but only to the minimum degree necessary. This is why its level equalled the subsistence minimum for the period November–December 1991.[4] After the valorisation of the minimum wage in January 1992, the minimum wage grew to 110% of the subsistence minimum, but in March 1993 it fell to 95%, and in January 1994 to 87%.

– The constant raising of the minimum wage seeks to address financial problems particularly in the sphere of state–owned enterprises. The productivity of these enterprises has fallen continuously.[5] The inability of enterprises to pay these wages on the one hand, and wage control as

---

[4] The official subsistence minimum for a single person was set by *Law No. 463/1991* from 1 November 1991 at CSK 1,700. Since it represents net income after tax, its level before tax is CSK 2,000. This subsistence minimum level remained unchanged until March 1993, when it was increased to CSK 1,960 (CSK 2,306 before tax).

[5] The management of some enterprises solved this by moving their employees to part–time jobs or by enforced leave (including unpaid) in periods of financial difficulty. Only some resorted to redundancies.

part of general government anti–inflationary policy on the other, would lead to the destruction of the wage tariff system and to the creation of a negative business environment for these enterprises. This offers one explanation for the fact that the Article of the General Agreement for 1991, concerning adjustment of the minimum wage to rises in the cost–of–living index (CLI), was not honoured. While the cost of living in 1991 increased by 40.7% in comparison with December 1990, the minimum wage was adjusted by only 10%, i.e. from CSK 2,000 to 2,200 (table 6.3).
– Moreover, the General Agreements for 1992, 1993 and 1994 did not include the above–mentioned Article concerning adjustment of the minimum wage to the level of the CLI, as a consequence of which there was a 27% fall in the real level of the minimum wage in the period following its first setting to the second quarter of 1993, from CSK 1,278 to 938. Note that the real average wage increased by 33% over the same period (table 6.1).

While at the beginning of 1992 the minimum wage was adjusted on the basis of consensus between government and trade unions (the trade unions understanding the need for an anti–inflationary policy in the transition period), the situation changed from 1993 to 1994. There are three factors motivating the Czech Government's desire to conserve the 1992 minimum wage level. First, low wage costs will maintain the comparative advantage of Czech products in Western markets. Second, minimum wage growth can lead to wage inflation. Third, from the beginning of 1993 the minimum wage has been the minimum base for the calculation of payments to the social and health insurance funds. These payments for some categories of citizens (e.g. for women on maternity leave, those on military service, and pensioners) are paid by the state. Public expenditure growth has been an additional argument against the demands of trade unions to increase the minimum wage at least to the subsistence minimum.

2. Minimum Wage and Low–Paid Workers

Figures relating to low–paid workers are important for an analysis of the effects of the minimum wage. In this section a more detailed analysis, both of those above and below the minimum wage level, is carried out. We calculated the percentage of workers earning:

– less than 12 CSK/hour (minimum wage level);
– less than 14 CSK/hour (45% of overall average wage, 48% of overall median);
– less than 20 CSK/hour (64% of overall average wage, 68% of overall median);
– less than 24 CSK/hour (77% of overall average wage, 82% of overall median).

Table 6.3 *The Development of the Cost of Living Index (CLI), the Minimum Wage and the Real Minimum Wage, Czech Republic, December 1990– June 1993*

	CLI 1989=100	CLI Dec 1990=100	Minimum wage in CSK	Real min.wage in CSK*
1990				
December	119.5	100.0	–	100.0
1991				
January	149.0	124.7	2 000	134.2
February	157.5	131.8	2 000	127.0
March	162.9	136.3	2 000	122.8
April	166.1	139.0	2 000	120.4
May	168.5	141.0	2 000	118.7
June	172.2	144.1	2 000	116.1
July	171.6	143.6	2 000	116.6
August	171.7	143.7	2 000	116.5
September	172.2	144.1	2 000	116.1
October	172.6	144.4	2 000	115.9
November	175.7	147.0	2 000	113.8
December	177.2	148.3	2 000	112.9
Average 1991	168.1	140.7	2 000	119.0
1992				
January	179.0	149.8	2 200	122.9
February	180.5	151.0	2 200	121.9
March	181.4	151.8	2 200	121.3
April	182.4	152.6	2 200	120.6
May	183.1	153.2	2 200	120.2
June	183.8	153.8	2 200	119.7
July	186.1	155.7	2 200	118.2
August	187.3	156.7	2 200	117.5
September	190.9	159.7	2 200	115.2
October	194.5	162.8	2 200	113.1
November	198.9	166.4	2 200	110.6
December	200.1	167.4	2 200	109.9
Average 1992	187.3	156.7	2 200	117.5
1993				
January	217.2	181.8	2 200	101.3
February	219.9	184.0	2 200	100.0
March	220.9	184.9	2 200	99.6
April	222.1	185.9	2 200	99.1
May	222.9	186.5	2 200	98.7
June	223.8	187.3	2 200	98.3
July	225.5	188.7	2 200	97.6
August	227.3	190.2	2 200	96.8
September	230.5	192.9	2 200	95.4
October	233.0	195.0	2 200	94.4
November	234.4	196.2	2 200	93.0
December	236.5	197.9	2 200	93.0
Average 1993	226.2	189.3	2 200	97.3

* Calculated as share of current minimum wage and current CLI, with the basic period Dec. 1990.
Source: Own computations, based on the data of the Czech Statistical Office.

Table 6.4 *Low Pay in Main Risk Groups, Czech Republic, 4th Quarter of 1992, (CSK)*

Group of workers	Average wage	Median wage	Percentage of workers earning less than (CSK/hour)			
			12	14	20	24
			minimum wage	50% of	2/3 of	80% of
					median wage	
Total workers	31.37	29.29	0.23	1.06	12.55	27.50
Workers aged 16–19	21.22	20.12	1.12	7.59	48.93	74.56
Workers aged 20–24	27.05	25.63	0.42	1.28	17.29	40.29
Female workers	25.50	24.43	0.44	1.70	22.85	47.45
Part–time workers	28.49	23.47	0.80	5.27	32.70	52.65
Female part–time workers	22.53	21.32	1.08	6.35	41.28	66.45

Source: Own computations, based on the Trexima Labour Cost Information System (ISCP).

The data, which come from the Labour Cost Information System, are based on average earnings for the 4th quarter of 1992. They provide us with a global picture of wage structure and low pay in the Czech Republic. These are the first available data concerning wage structures since the beginning of the economic reform process. As can be seen from table 6.4 only a negligible percentage of workers (0.23%) earn less than the minimum wage (CSK 12).

According to our data the minimum wage represents only 41% of the overall median wage. This level of minimum wage is considerably lower than in developed countries, where it represents above 60% of the median wage.[6]

Analysing data from table 6.4, we can say that the lowest–paid group is that of workers aged 16–19, especially female workers, representing about 38% of low paid workers in this age category.[7] The fact that very young people had lower earnings is not to be explained as a negative factor however. Being low– or unskilled workers with fewer qualifications and less experience they have more difficulty finding a job than other workers. On the other hand, their low earnings give them a comparative advantage. With age, the likelihood of low–pay tends to diminish up to the age of 61, after which it begins to rise again.[8] •The second high risk group is the small

---

[6] S. Bazen and G. Benhayoun: 'Low Pay and Wage Regulations in the European Community', *British Journal of Industrial Relations*, December 1992.

[7] A. Buchtikova (1993): 'The Empirical Analysis of the Wage Structure and the Effects of Minimum Wages in the Period of Transformation: The Case of the Czech Republic', Paper presented at the International Conference on the Economic Analysis of Low Pay and the Effects of Minimum Wages. Arles, France, 30 September–1 October. Part–time workers are also likely to be low paid, but the proportion of these two groups is not high.

[8] Buchtikova (1993) op. cit., At the same time, the position of part–time workers and women, whether full– or part–time, is worse for all age groups.

Table 6.5 *Low Pay by Sector, Czech Republic, Last Quarter of 1992 (CSK)*

Group of workers	Average wage	Median wage	\multicolumn{4}{c}{Percentage of workers earning less than (CSK/hour)}			
			12	14	20	24
•			minimum wage	50% of	2/3 of	80% of
					median wage	
Total workers	31.37	29.29	0.23	1.06	12.55	27.50
Metallurgy	36.78	36.28	0.01	0.21	4.20	11.27
Chemistry	33.76	31.64	0.06	0.15	7.73	20.97
Engineering	28.72	27.75	0.20	1.19	16.22	32.40
Electronics	28.32	27.06	0.63	1.90	14.12	32.57
Woodworking	24.47	23.96	0.57	2.83	27.83	50.32
Rubber	34.89	31.86	0.07	0.46	8.23	22.16
Pulp and paper	31.37	28.93	0.00	1.66	17.34	32.11
Textile	25.92	25.10	0.23	1.37	18.31	42.31
Food	25.18	23.15	2.93	5.40	31.36	55.04
Building materials	29.38	29.42	0.00	0.00	0.00	6.12
Construction	26.01	24.58	0.35	1.93	20.32	45.18
Forestry	44.69	43.73	0.00	0.00	0.00	0.00
Water supply	25.99	27.28	0.00	6.02	30.56	35.65
Agriculture	24.48	23.25	0.56	2.25	29.73	54.39
Transport	24.83	24.10	0.33	2.29	26.31	49.67
Publishing and printing	28.82	25.08	0.00	0.00	19.29	43.93
Trade	41.02	38.38	0.00	1.03	3.10	8.53
Services	36.06	30.30	0.00	5.59	11.89	20.89

Source: Own computations, based on the Trexima Labour Cost Information System (ISCP).

group of part–time workers. Once again women tend to be predominant. Indeed, women account for above 60% of low–paid workers overall.

For a more detailed picture of the structure of low–paid workers a sectoral analysis has been carried out. The large percentages of low–paid workers in certain sectors (table 6.5) must be explained. Some are characterised by low productivity or employ low–skilled workers. Type of industry is also important. Traditionally, wages in 'heavy industries' are higher than in 'light industries'.

The largest number of low–paid workers are in the food industry, though the following sectors are also characterised by low pay: engineering, electronics, woodworking, pulp and paper, textiles, construction, water, agriculture, transport, and publishing and printing.[9]

[9] J. Hlaváček's team at the Institute of Economics of the Czechoslovak Academy of Sciences. In 1992 minimum wage tariffs in agriculture could be about 15% lower (see *Government Directive No. 43/1992*), but workers in this sector are also able to obtain so–called 'income in kind'. From the beginning of 1993, this exception was terminated.

3. The Impact of Minimum Wage Growth on Levels of Employment

As outlined above, the permanent valorisation of the value of the minimum wage is designed to address financial problems arising in connection with former or currently state–owned enterprises. It is of course highly likely that a number of low–profit or unprofitable sectors with a high proportion of low–paid workers would not be able to absorb minimum wage rises without reducing employment levels. The implications of a rise in the minimum wage for enterprises in financial difficulties as regards employment levels were calculated using data from the Labour Cost Information System and from the databases of individual Czech enterprises in two stages.

First, I calculated the expected growth in the total wage bill (D WB$_i$) if the national minimum wage was increased to the following levels: CSK 13, CSK 14, CSK 16, CSK 18, CSK 20, CSK 22 and CSK 24, with the formula:

$$D\ WB_i = (\ w_{min\ i} - w_{a\ 12}\ ) * L_{1992} * \%L_{12} * F\ /\ WB_{1992}$$

D WB$_i$:   *expected growth of the total wage bill;*
$w_{min\ i}$:   *new adjusted level of the national minimum wage;*
$w_{a\ 12}$:   *average wage in the categories which are paid today at a level below the new hypothetical minimum wage* ($w_{min\ i}$);
L_{1992}:   *total number of employees in 1992;*
$\%L_{12}$:   *proportion of employees paid less than the new hypothetical* $w_{min\ i}$ *wage;*
F: *yearly fund of working hours;*
WB_{1992}:   *total wage bill in 1992.*

Table 6.6 presents the results of the first step in the calculation of the expected increase in the wage bill due to the adjustment of the minimum wage to the

Table 6.6 *Expected Wage Bill Growth Due to Adjustment of the Minimum Wage, Czech Republic, 1992 (%)*

	13 CSK	14 CSK	16 CSK	18 CSK	20 CSK	22 CSK	24 CSK
Metallurgy	0.002	0.007	0.035	0.118	0.315	0.670	1.256
Chemistry	0.003	0.007	0.055	0.224	0.609	1.306	2.477
Engineering	0.029	0.062	0.245	0.742	1.723	3.273	5.434
Electronics	0.040	0.096	0.312	0.751	1.631	3.147	5.460
Woodworking	0.052	0.142	0.602	1.784	3.820	6.759	10.663
Rubber	0.005	0.015	0.063	0.216	0.602	1.368	2.609
Pulp and paper	0.005	0.028	0.243	0.739	1.779	3.365	5.528
Textiles	0.030	0.083	0.323	0.969	2.296	4.603	8.074
Food	0.396	0.589	1.174	2.290	4.258	7.195	11.021
Building materials	0.000	0.000	0.000	0.000	0.000	0.081	0.373
Construction	0.053	0.104	0.323	0.830	1.936	3.789	6.512
Total	0.024	0.052	0.189	0.540	1.258	2.456	4.226

Source: Own computations, based on the Trexima Labour Cost Information System (ISCP), 1992.

level $w_{min\,i}$ for all new hypothetical levels of $w_{min\,i}$. The greater impact of the adjustment of the minimum wage on the rise in the wage bill can be observed in food, woodworking, textiles and construction. There would also be a considerable impact in engineering, electronics, and pulp and paper.

In the second step, the expected impact of a rise in the total wage bill on employment levels is tested using a simple econometric model. This model uses the above–calculated wage rise and information from individual Czech state–owned enterprises. It estimates an additional increase in unemployment as the result of a minimum wage–led increase in the wage bill. A similar model was first used in 1990 for the quantification of the impact of minimum wage and material cost increases on employment levels.[10]

The model quantifies the demand for labour power at each enterprise on the basis of simplified budget constraint:

$$P = (w_a * n) + c$$

P: *gross output*;
w_a: *average wage at this firm*;
n: *number of employees*;
c: *non–wage costs (mostly financial and material costs)*.

Operation within this budget constraint is the basic condition for the survival of the enterprise. When we fix 'P' and 'c' we can analyse the impact of the rise in the wage bill ($w_a * n$) on the level of employment. Put simply, if an enterprise is having financial problems or cannot find a market for an increasing volume of its production, the wage bill of this enterprise can be increased only at the expense of profits. The necessary corollary of this is that redundancies are inevitable if profitability is to be maintained. Moreover, only a certain portion of the workforce can be let go. This portion is given by the level of employment below which the enterprise loses the ability to continue operations and so faces closure. This 'overemployment' was estimated in the model as being one–third of all employees.

At the beginning of the calculation the basic level of the reduction in workforce—percentage share of discharged workers of the original number of employees in the sector—at loss–making firms is calculated. After that the additional reduction caused by the increased wage bill is computed. The model uses enterprise data, profits, wage costs, average wage and number of employees, calculated before the rise of the wage bill for the sector as a whole (table 6.6). The results of computations for all enterprises are presented in table 6.7.

The original model assumed employers would make redundant all categories of workers, but in fact they chose low–paid and low–skilled workers.

[10] For more information see A. Capek: 'The Variants of Czecho–Slovak Economic Relations', research study prepared for the Czech Government, 1991.

Table 6.7 *Wage and Employment Effects of Minimum Wage Growth, Czech Republic, 1992 (%)*

New level of minimum wage	Rise of wage bill	Reduction in no. of employees	Additional reduction
		12.98*	
13 CSK	0.024	12.98	0.00
14 CSK	0.052	12.98	0.00
16 CSK	0.189	13.08	0.10
18 CSK	0.540	13.10	0.12
20 CSK	1.258	13.15	0.17
22 CSK	2.456	13.37	0.39
24 CSK	4.226	13.84	0.85

* Basic level of reduction in no. of employees.

Table 6.8 *Effects of Minimum Wage Growth on Low–Paid Workers, Czech Republic, 1992 (%)*

New level of minimum wage	Rise of wage bill	Reduction in no. of employees	Additional reduction
		17.20	
13 CSK	0.024	17.89	0.69
14 CSK	0.052	17.93	0.73
16 CSK	0.189	18.34	1.14
18 CSK	0.540	18.67	1.47
20 CSK	1.258	19.15	2.30
22 CSK	2.456	21.30	4.10

Thus, in table 6.7 the minimum effect of the rise in the minimum wage is presented. If we assume the redundancy of lower–paid workers, for example earning 80% of average wages, growth in unemployment will, of course, be higher (table 6.8).

As can be seen from tables 6.7 and 6.8 the further reduction of the work-force in connection with a rise in the minimum wage is lower than that due to an enterprise's financial difficulties. At the same time, a combination of these two factors can lead to an even greater reduction in the levels of low–paid workers in some sectors.

The aim of the following analysis is to compare the abilities of the vari-ous industrial sectors to absorb a rise in the minimum wage without having to resort to redundancies. The analysis is based on a comparison between the basic level of redundancies, the financial situation of the various sectors and the average additional rise in redundancies due to a 1% rise of the wage bill.[11]

[11] This indicator was computed as the slope of the regression curve with the minimum additional reduction as a variable dependent on wage bill growth.

Table 6.9 *Effects of a 1% Wage Bill Rise Due to Minimum Wage Growth, Czech Republic, 1992 (%)*

Sector	Basic level of employment reduction	Further emp. reduction due to 1% rise in WB	Average monthly wage (CSK)	Value added/ employee (CSK 1,000)	Proportn. of profit in wage bill	Proportn. of bad debt in equity	Proportn. of part–time workers
Metallurgy	15.31	0.236	5 677	104.708	0.54	0.161	3.35
Chemistry	1.21	0.104	5 323	262.085	3.10	0.039	0.85
Engineering	19.31	0.598	4 649	65.817	0.18	0.214	1.72
Electronics	26.93	0.679	4 216	58.900	0.16	0.213	2.61
Wood ind.	5.74	0.615	4 081	68.911	0.41	0.101	3.35
Rubber	7.73	0.453	5 234	118.224	0.88	0.037	2.30
Pulp/paper	18.35	0.481	4 697	84.363	0.50	0.051	0.95
Textiles	11.16	0.705	3 720	56.631	0.27	0.128	6.34
Food	–	–	4 645	88.330	1.58	–	1.89
Building materials	6.71	0.363	4 803	111.578	0.94	0.025	0.00
Construction	4.42	0.687	5 076	80.945	0.33	0.068	2.28
Total	12.98	0.546	4 668	84.246	0.50	0.138	2.94

Source: Own computations, based on the Trexima Labour Cost Information System (ISCP) and data from individual state–owned enterprises.

The worst financial situation, low value added per employee, low proportion of profit in wage bill, high proportion of bad debts in equity, is observed in the electronics industry, engineering, textiles and the woodworking industry (table 6.9). These sectors, along with the food industry, would not be able to absorb a rise in the minimum wage without a reduction in their workforce.

4. Conclusion

The minimum wage in the Czech Republic in the period of transformation (1989–1993) has a number of characteristic features. It protects employees only to a limited degree and its adjustment does not correspond to increases in the cost of living. Moreover, its relative level, expressed as a proportion of the average wage, is on a steadily downward trend. On the other hand, all workers are covered by minimum wage protection and only a negligible portion of them (0.23%) earn less than the minimum wage.

Considering the poor financial situation of industrial enterprises in the Czech Republic we might have expected that it would be difficult for them to absorb rises in the minimum wage without corresponding redundancies. Our analysis started with the assumption that enterprises are operating under severe budgetary constraints and that management will be forced to dismiss part of the workforce or face bankruptcy. Today enterprises are maintaining overemployment and only a small number of unprofitable firms have become bankrupt since 1989. This being the case, we can conclude that the role of the rise of the minimum wage in increasing unemployment is not as significant as might have been expected. This fact was further confirmed by the results of our calculations. While the basic level of the reduction of the workforce, consequent upon the current financial situation of the firm represents approximately 13%, additional reductions as a result of the upward adjustment of the minimum wage by 50%, to the level of 18 CSK/hour, represent only 0.12% of the current number of employees.

Higher levels of redundancy may be expected if we assume dismissal of low–paid workers, but even in this case the additional reduction of the workforce is not high.

The results of our analysis lead to the conclusion that a constant raising of the minimum wage will not necessarily cause a substantial increase in the rate of unemployment. At the same time, in certain sectors, such as electronics, engineering, textiles, food, and the woodworking industry, it is much more difficult to absorb rises in the minimum wage. Low–paid female workers in the textile and food industries are especially threatened by unemployment.

7

Minimum Wages and Collective Bargaining in Bulgaria

Todor Radev[*]

1. Introduction

Wage policy and, more specifically, the minimum wage in Bulgaria were for years constrained by the ideological framework of the communist socio–economic system. The centrally planned economy made it possible to maintain low wage levels alongside a great number of widely available social benefits and possibilities to purchase on a non–market basis, regulated by party and government bodies. The well–being of the people depended more on social and political status and degree of submission than professional qualifications and economic performance.

The general wage level was extremely low, and differentials minimal. Low wage levels were essentially the price that had to be paid for maintaining full employment in the centrally planned economy. Ideologically, it was desirable for the Party to maintain high overemployment (between 15% and 25%), thereby eliminating a possible source of social discontent.

Such an approach was possible due to the lack of a direct relation between productivity (too low because of overmanning) and wages, the nonexistence of collective bargaining and the passive role of the trade unions.

The wage system inherited from the centralised economy turned out to be entirely inadequate in the transition to a market economy, not only because of its separation from results and productivity, but also because of the lack of a compensating mechanism for inflation.

2. The Minimum Wage within the Wage Bargaining System

In the 1980s a weak attempt was made to update the wage system with the more extensive use of various piece–rate and bonus mechanisms applying to both workers and management at all levels. The low level of inflation, however, and regular wage rate increases kept wages at a constant, if low level. One of the main aims of the central authorities was to keep wage

* Institute of Economics, Bulgarian Academy of Sciences.

differentials to a minimum both within a single sector and between sectors. Physical labour was given priority over intellectual labour.

After the liberalisation of prices at the beginning of 1991, the wage system encountered the need to compensate the high inflation for the first time (over 250% in March in comparison to January).[1] This had first been publicly discussed at the end of 1989. An important element in the creation of a modern wage system was the acceptance of collective bargaining. A special tripartite commission for interest reconciliation was established in September 1991. In July of the same year *Decree No. 123 of the Council of Ministers* introduced a wage bargaining system between the social partners.

The principle scheme for wage bargaining envisaged two main levels: national and enterprise. Sectoral and regional level wage bargaining were also made possible on request.

In 1991 and 1992, however, collective agreements were mainly concluded at national and enterprise level. The main reasons for the small scale of sectoral level bargaining were unwillingness on the part of ministries and the delay and difficult formation of the respective tripartite commissions for social partnership. The lack of sectoral level bargaining also had a negative effect on the wage bargaining system. On the one hand, employees were not in a position to negotiate because they had no experience. On the other hand, higher wage levels were needed as soon as possible, because of delayed bargaining at national level and high inflation. Eventually, this resulted in a peculiar form of centralisation of collective bargaining: what was agreed at national level predetermined the scope of more decentralised bargaining. What would normally be considered proper to sectoral level bargaining was transferred to national level (for instance, the wages of all those employed in the principal budget–financed sectors).

As far as the minimum wage is concerned, the system presupposes national level bargaining of the main principles and criteria for its formation, and minimum wage rates and the conditions and means for their modification. The minimum wage agreed at national level thereby becomes the obligatory minimum at sectoral and local level. The firm is obliged to pay the minimum wage approved in the collective contract even when there are no resources for paying wages, results are poor, etc.

At the beginning of 1991 the National Tripartite Commission accepted the proposal of the trade union CL Podkrepa to determine the minimum wage according to the rate of the social minimum,[2] without allowing it to

[1] All figures in this paper are taken from or recalculated on the basis of official data, published by the National Statistical Institute and the Ministry of Labour and Social Welfare.
[2] The social minimum is determined with the help of a consumer basket containing 600 goods and services necessary for meeting the minimum physical, intellectual and social needs of a single person. It is calculated and published monthly by the National Statistical Institute according to methods approved by the social partners.

fall below 70% of that minimum. The idea was to circumvent the sharp decline of the minimum wage in real terms, which had already shrunk from 78.4% of the social minimum in 1989 to 71.4% of this minimum in 1990. Unfortunately, this could not be achieved: during the period from September 1990 to March 1993, only in June and July 1991 was the minimum wage in Bulgaria a little over 70% of the social minimum. A year later, in June 1992, the minimum wage amounted only to 32.1% of the social minimum. It turned out that the Government had signed an agreement that was difficult to realise mainly on two counts: first, the decline in the average wage was so great that, from February until September, the average wage was actually lower than the social minimum. The minimum wage reached about 80% of the average wage, which was unsustainable due to the heterogeneity of labour conditions and results; second, the normative relation of the minimum wage to a number of social benefits—pensions, grants, family allowances, unemployment benefits, etc. Any increase in the minimum wage required several times greater coverage for these social payments. In the middle of 1991 an attempt to reach a compromise was made with the introduction of the so–called 'starting wage' parallel to the minimum wage, although they were in fact equal for all workers. Later on, the Government terminated the link between the minimum wage and the social minimum.

In April 1993 the social partners agreed on a reassessment of the minimum wage to be carried out every three months, compensating 90% of actual inflation growth. At the end of the year the Government rejected this formula and at the beginning of 1994 introduced inflation forecasts as a base for the calculation of compensation, to the detriment of employees. The implementation of this base divided the trade unions: CL Podkrepa refused to sign the agreement, CITUB signed it. In Autumn 1994, however, one of the demands of the national warning strike announced by CITUB was the revival of actual inflation as a base for the calculation of compensation.

Sectoral level bargaining had a broad base for the first time during collective bargaining in 1993. In almost all sectors, a higher minimum wage was envisaged as compared to the one agreed at national level. This was natural considering the relatively low level that the minimum wage had reached and the desire of each sector to do better (in many sectors wage scales are based on the minimum wage). The greater part of sectoral contracts now take the minimum wage as a coefficient of the minimum wage agreed at national level and envisage that it should increase in tandem. In the other sectoral contracts the minimum wage is fixed, but there are mechanisms to update it in accordance with inflation (table 7.1).

The statistical study (census) carried out by the National Statistical Institute on the level of wages in various sectors in October 1993 shows the

Table 7.1 *The Agreed Minimum Wage and the Percentage Share of Employees Receiving the Minimum Wage or Below, Bulgaria, 1993*

Sectors and subsectors	From	Minimum wage	% of employees •on the minimum wage*or below‡ Oct–93
Electricity and thermal power	1–Jan–93	1.4†	0.20‡
Coal	1–Apr–93	1 800	0.00‡
Ferrous metallurgy	1–Apr–93	1.3†	0.70‡
Nonferrous metallurgy	1–Apr–93	1.3†	0.70‡
Machine–building and metal–cutting	1–Mar–93	1 350	1.80*
Chemical and oil–processing	1–Jan–93	1 500	0.60*
Wood and wood products	1–Apr–93	1 250	5.60*
Pulp and paper	1–Jan–93	1 350	4.30*
Textiles	1–May–93	1 400	4.60*
Clothing	1–May–93	1 400	21.90*
Leather and footwear	1–May–93	1 400	14.50*
Printing and publishing	1–Apr–93	1 500	1.50*
Food, beverages, tobacco	1–Jan–93	1 800	2.80‡
Construction	1–Jan–93	1.3†	6.50‡
Transport	1–Jan–93	1 400	2.30*
Communications	1–Jan–93	1 943	1.50‡
Trade	19–Mar–93	1.3†	24.30‡
Tourist industry	1–Jan–93	1.4†	6.30‡

† A coefficient of the national minimum wage.
The national minimum wage was increased to 1,200 levs in March 1993, to 1,343 levs in July 1993, and to 1,414 levs in October 1993.
Source: National Statistical Institute.

true situation. It turns out that, similarly to national minimum wage bargaining, what was agreed was very different from what was actually paid. According to the data available, table 7.1 presents, for each sector of the economy, the minimum wage agreed at sectoral level and gives the percentage of workers in that sector who are paid at the minimum wage level or even below. The percentage of employees paid below the agreed minimum wage is particularly striking in trade (nearly 25%), but also in construction (6.5%), the tourist industry (6.3%), and the food industry (2.8%). A high percentage of employees in the clothing (21.9%), the leather and footwear (14.5%), and the wood industries (5.6%) are paid at the agreed minimum wage. The percentage of people receiving less than the national minimum wage in October 1993 has been given for the collective contracts with a fixed minimum wage. The respective sectoral minimum wages, however, should be higher, especially in the coal and mining industry, telecommunications, the food industry, etc. Almost four years of collective bargaining at national, sectoral and enterprise level have indicated that ineffectiveness is the major weakness of the Bulgarian bargaining system. The reasons for this include the unexpectedly long economic crisis, a lack of interest in higher productivity on the part of labour, and management failures in state enterprises. The ineffectiveness of collective bargaining is only matched by its constantly decreasing scope, since the number of people employed in the state sector is rapidly shrinking, and there is as yet no collective bargaining in the private sector.

3. The Erosion of the Minimum Wage in Real Terms

When analysing the influence of changes in the minimum wage on such macroeconomic phenomena as inflation and unemployment, we must always take into consideration the mechanisms already described for minimum wage bargaining in Bulgaria. There are, however, a number of other peculiarities in Bulgarian economic and social reality which should also be taken into consideration if we want this analysis to be accurate.

Comparing, for example, trends in the monthly changes of the minimum wage and inflation, a certain synchrony could be discerned, especially with reference to data from 1991. Thus, in February 1991 as compared to January of the same year, the minimum wage increased 1.85 times, and inflation 2.23 times. As with subsequent increases, this relates mainly to compensation through minimum and other wage levels for the rise in the cost of living due to the price liberalisation of some goods and services. Bearing in mind that these wage increases were paid with a delay of up to 2 or 3 months, after comparing the data it will clearly be seen that the rise in inflation preceded the rise in wages.

In other words, we can hardly speak of serious problems regarding an increase of the minimum wage over the rate of inflation, although other wages and social security benefits always increased along with it. The very means of compensating wages—taking place less often but involving larger amounts usually paid in a lump sum and including arrears—created conditions favourable for inflationary pressure, but this did not materialise and was neutralised in the following months. One of the reasons for this is the fact—alluded to at the beginning of the chapter—that wage income in Bulgaria represents a comparatively small share, about one–third, of all income, and this share is constantly decreasing. Another indication of the insignificant inflationary role of wages is the relatively small share of wages in production costs (13.3% in industry in 1992). In addition, the minimum wage represents only 3% of this already small share of wages, so that we can expect that an increase in the minimum wage would have only a small effect on wage costs and an even smaller effect on total production costs.[3]

Together with the insignificant and decreasing share of the minimum wage overall, for the last four to five years there has been a sharp fall in the net minimum wage in real terms. According to our calculations, in 1989 the purchasing power of the minimum wage in Bulgaria was about 25% lower as compared to the end of 1970s. If we take 1989 as the base year (=100), by 1990 the real minimum wage had decreased to 94.6, in 1991 to 59.8, in 1992 to 41.8 and in 1993 to 40.7.[4] It is evident that in only four years the minimum wage in real terms fell by 2.5 times.

The discrepancies between the increase of the minimum wage and the increase of inflation are illustrated in figure 7.1. While the inflation curve is steep and represents a comparatively stable increasing tendency, the increase of the nominal minimum wage is more irregular. At the same time, the figure clearly shows that the increase of the minimum wage compared to retail price growth is much slower.

Since September 1991, as a result of collective bargaining and the fact that real wages had reached an extremely low level (the average wage was lower than the social minimum for a working person), the real wage showed a tendency towards rapid increase. This did not compensate lost purchasing power, but created a certain inflationary potential, so that the Government implemented an even more restrictive income policy, based on the central regulation of wage fund increases; levying a progressive tax on wage fund increases, with the aim of limiting wage growth, particularly in industry. Once the Government determined national norms for wage funds in consultation with trade unions, enterprises had to fix wage increases accordingly; those that distributed a wage fund above the limit had to pay a progressive tax, the top rate being 400% for an increase of the wage bill of 4% above the ceiling. The progressive tax scale was reduced again, the top rate remaining 400% but only applicable if the wage fund exceeded a ceiling of 6% growth. The excess wage tax was henceforth to be paid regardless of the enterprise's profitability. Initially, wage fund norms were to be set annually, but in early 1991 *Decree No. 24* specified that wage fund norms were to be adjusted at the end of each quarter, and were supposed to take account of price increases, changes in average nominal wages and productivity.

The effectiveness of this measure for controlling inflation is questionable. As there was no penalty for unpaid tax, several enterprises did not

[3] For a description of percentages by industry, see Chapter 3 of *The Bulgarian Challenge: Reforming Labour Market and Social Policy*, ILO Country Objectives Review No. 1 (Budapest, ILO–CEET, 1993).
[4] Calculated on the basis of monthly inflation figures, published by the National Statistical Institute.

Figure 7. 1 *Nominal Minimum Wage and Price Index, Bulgaria, 1990–94 (Levs)*

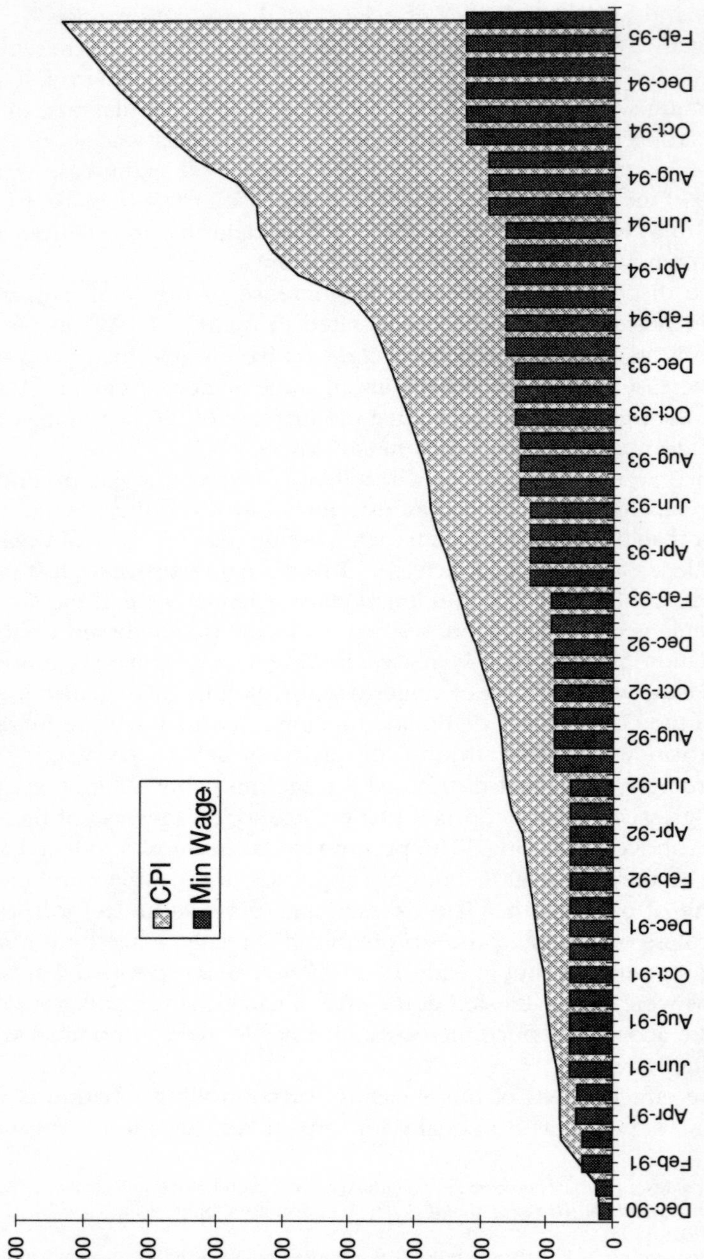

Source: National Statistical Institute

pay (in fact only 31% of taxes were paid). With this policy, nominal wages lagged well behind consumer prices and real wages fell by more than 42% in 1991. Although wages more than kept pace with prices in 1992, a real wage increase of about 14% was insufficient to compensate for the reduction suffered in 1991. In 1994, they experienced a new fall.

Nominal wages rose in profitable sectors, such as finance and banking, those with sharp employment cuts (industry) and transport and communication. The decrease in real wages was also important in agriculture and in the clothing and textile industries.[5]

The reduction of real wages in these sectors was 15 to 40% higher than the average reduction from 1990 to 1993. It is worth noting that the largest decreases in real wages can be observed in sectors in which they were relatively low to begin with.

Just the opposite is the case in sectors where average wages are relatively high: in the financial sector and the production of electricity and thermal power 1990 real wage levels have been maintained or even increased. In addition, lower declines in real wages can be observed in ferrous metallurgy, chemicals and crude oil extraction, glass and china, and printing and publishing. Devaluation in these sectors is one–third to three–quarters lower than the average.

Regarding the minimum wage, two opposite tendencies in the decrease of real wages are maintained. In sectors where real wages are declining more rapidly the share of workers receiving the minimum wage is growing; in sectors where real wage reduction is smaller, the share of workers receiving the minimum wage or close to it is diminishing.

Two examples must suffice here. In science, the share of employees receiving the minimum wage increased from 1.2% in June 1990 to 3.2% in October 1993. In finance, credit and insurance the share of employees receiving the minimum wage decreased from 3.1% to 0.5% during the same period.

4. Scope and Sectoral Distribution of the Minimum Wage

The number of employed persons receiving the minimum wage decreased steadily: from 128,000 in 1989 to 106,000 in 1990, 91,000 in 1991, 73,000 in 1992 and 52,000 in 1993. The figures only cover those employed with a labour contract for a full month in state enterprises and cooperatives. This is the main reason for the decrease in the absolute number of people receiving the minimum wage, since the number of those employed in the

---

[5] See Chapter 3 of ILO–CEET Report, 1993, op. cit.

state sector declined in the period in question by over half. The relative share of people receiving the minimum wage was stable, fluctuating between 3.3% and 3.6%. The number of people receiving the minimum wage in 1993 was larger if certain peculiarities in the study carried out by the National Statistical Institute are taken into consideration. First, there are no data for agriculture and forestry, where the share of people on minimum wages is traditionally high—between 8% and 14%, or about 25,000 people. In accordance with the limits imposed on wage bills many companies use so–called civil contracts to avoid penalty taxes. It seems that a certain percentage of those without labour contracts and part–time workers get wages close to or lower than the minimum. Mothers on paid maternity leave receive the minimum wage and number about 110,000. There are also those on involuntary unpaid leave (about 35–50,000). In other words, at least 250,000, or almost 10% of the working population, receive the minimum or a lower wage, usually those with low qualifications and young, inexperienced workers. According to the existing wage system in Bulgaria for each year of working experience wages increase by a minimum 0.6%; that is, an employee with over 16 years of experience receives a wage at least 10% above the minimum.

We have estimated that about 85–90% of workers on the minimum wage have low qualifications, and the rest are mostly security guards, porters, nightwatchmen or support personnel (mainly retired people). Furthermore, at least three–quarters of these workers are women.

The statistical information on the sectoral distribution of those receiving the minimum wage is quite inadequate. Table 7.2 gives the official statistical data for 1990–93, according to which the total share of those receiving the minimum wage in the state and cooperative sector fell from 3.5% in 1990 to 3.3% in 1993.

Unfortunately, we do not have data for 1993 by specific industries, and also agriculture and forestry were not included in the survey.

Table 7.2, however, shows that the highest increase in the relative share of those on the minimum wage was in the sectors most seriously affected by unemployment: industry, trade, transport, science, public health, etc. An opposite tendency may be discerned in the financial sector and in administration.

The 1993 statistical survey also includes subsectoral data. The subsectors with the highest share of those on the minimum wage are the following: clothing (29%), public utilities (18.8%), leather, fur and shoes (14.5%), and other small subsectors with a share of about 20%.

At the opposite end of the scale are coal mining, oil, ferrous metallurgy, and electric and thermal energy, in which the percentage of those on minimum wages is below 0.1%.

Table 7.2 *Share of Employed Receiving the Minimum Wage, Bulgaria, 1990–93*

Year	1990	1993
Total	3.50	3.30
Industry	2.80	3.90
Electricity and thermal power	0.10	–
Coal	–	0.0
Crude oil extraction	–	0.0
Ferrous metallurgy	–	0.0
Nonferrous metallurgy	–	0.20
Machine–building and metal–cutting	–	1.80
Electrical and electronic	–	3.60
Chemical and oil–processing	–	0.60
Industry of building materials	–	1.00
Wood and wood products	–	5,60
Pulp and paper	–	4.3
Glass, china	–	0.90
Textiles	–	14.60
Clothing	–	21.90
Leather and footwear	–	14.50
Printing and publishing	–	1.50
Food, beverages, tobacco	–	1.10
Other	–	25.60
Construction	1.20	1.90
Agriculture	7.5	–
Forestry	5.8	–
Transport	1.60	2.30
Communications	0.70	0.50
Trade	3.80	8.00
Other material production	2.20	2.30
Housing, communal services	2.90	4.30
Science	1.20	3.20
Education	3.00	2.10
Culture	4.10	3.80
Health	1.40	1.70
Finance, credit, insurance	3.10	0.50
Administration	1.30	0.60
Other	7.50	–

Source: National Statistical Institute.

These great differences in respect of the fixed minimum wage in light and heavy industry cannot be justified. Neither the shares of low–qualified workers in the two subsectors nor labour intensity differ substantially.

The explanation lies in the specifics of the monopolistic energy and mining industries. They are not directly subject to market forces. This is why the shrinkage of their domestic and international markets has not been as dramatic as for light industry. Another important factor is the better organisation of trade unions in heavy industry giving them an advantage in wage negotiations.

5. The Influence of the Minimum Wage on Pay Differentials

The changes in wage levels have influenced pay differentials above all. For years there was a policy of relatively small variations in wages among sectors and between high and low paid employees. For example, if we compare the 10% of employees earning the highest wages with the 10% earning the lowest, we can easily see to what extent minimum wage policy has influenced pay differentials in the public and cooperative spheres.

Until 1989 this differentiation was less than three times and the minimum wage, along with other wages, increased rather seldom, and without any significant change in the correlation between them. However, with the beginning of the transition to a market economy (mainly with price liberalisation and collective bargaining) changes became more dynamic. In June 1990 high paid workers received about 3.6 times the wages of low paid workers.

At the first negotiations on minimum wages and ways to compensate inflation–hit incomes, the major concern was to protect mainly those with low wages. The minimum wage was raised from 235 levs in January 1991 to 435 levs in February and 620 levs in June. The relatively high minimum wage reduced the difference between high and low wages to less than 2.5 times for February–May 1991. Then for a long period the minimum wage and other wages close to it remained relatively stable. As a result only a year later (in June 1994) the difference between high and low wages had increased to almost five times. With certain fluctuations this remained the case until March 1994. The National Statistical Institute study in October 1993 showed a difference of 4.8 times between the highest 10% of wage earners and the lowest 10%.

Analysing the employment changes in the various sectors, and proceeding from the available data on the size of the minimum and average wages (insofar as the minimum wage and its relative share is a function of the average wage) in various sectors, certain correlations can be discerned.

Most impressive is the considerable differentiation in the average wage in the various sectors for the period 1990–93 (table 7.3). In 1990 the average wage in the coal mining industry was 1.8 times greater than the lowest average wage, in forestry. In the second quarter of 1993 those employed in the coal mining industry still had the highest average wage, but it was now 3.3 times higher than the lowest average wage, in the clothing industry, and 2.7 or 2.8 times higher than the average wage in forestry and agriculture.

Table 7.3 *Sectoral and Subsectoral Differentiation of Average Wages, Bulgaria, 1989–93*

Year	1989	1990	1991	1992	1993
Total	274	361	959	1 895	3 144
Industry	290	350	964	2 017	3 404
Electricity and thermal power	332	462	1 418	3 646	5 621
Coal	395	535	1 469	3 476	5 579
Crude oil extraction	359	425	1 255	2 557	3 882
Ferrous metallurgy	373	460	1 263	3 181	5 170
Non–ferrous metallurgy	395	478	1 265	2 884	4 737
Machine–building and metal–cutting	305	359	974	2 004	3 162
Electrical and electronic	285	318	837	1 644	2 706
Chemical and oil–processing	328	394	1 257	2 935	4 583
Building materials	299	370	1 030	2 089	3 455
Wood and wood products	280	333	901	1 698	2 583
Pulp and paper	248	289	832	1 682	2 857
Glass, china	296	365	883	1 773	2 946
Textiles	264	312	772	1 507	2 385
Clothing	218	271	637	1 198	2 006
Leather and footwear	260	308	819	1 545	2 302
Printing and publishing	285	353	1 159	2 236	4 199
Food, beverages, tobacco	256	337	1 013	2 201	3 547
Other	243	288	614	1 037	1 610
Construction	306	397	1 119	2 215	3 244
Agriculture	269	405	939	1 425	2 221
Forestry	236	287	771	1 418	2 124
Transport	298	389	1 048	2 320	3 830
Communications	253	346	1 005	2 064	3 344
Trade	232	312	862	1 797	2 983
Other material production	295	356	1 072	2 395	3 716
Housing, communal services	246	326	953	1 974	3 127
Science	310	385	975	1 886	2 911
Education	231	322	876	1 591	2 604
Culture	245	313	843	1 499	2 560
Health	225	351	885	1 665	2 778
Finance, credit, insurance	268	385	1 344	3 084	6 207
Administration	296	398	1 067	2 078	3 668
Other	257	344	898	1 933	3 507
Standard deviation	46	59	208	634	1 094

Source: National Statistical Institute.

Average wages (and the minimum wage) have reached the highest levels in industries where there have been rises in the number of those employed. Thus, the number of those employed in finance, credit and insurance increased 11.2% as compared to 1991, and the average wage in the sector 13.6 times.

On the other hand, the greatest relative decrease in the average wage is in sectors with the highest relative and absolute numbers of people laid–off: agriculture, light industry, construction, science, the electrical and electronics industry.[6]

There are a number of deviations from the above trend, but they may be easily explained. For example, in many budget–financed sectors (education, health, management), the number of those employed remains unchanged or falls slightly, while the average wage relatively declines. However, these are sectors in which market forces do not operate, and redundancies are limited by the impossibility of cutting particular services. In other sectors, such as food and beverages, printing and publishing, housing and commerce, the increase in the average and minimum wages is the result of a considerable decrease in the number of those employed by about one–third (over one–half in commerce). Despite relatively good operating conditions, these industries had to scale down their labour costs in order to compete with the private sector and import liberalisation.

No doubt, enforced redundancies as well as the attainment of particular levels of average and minimum wages are influenced by many additional factors. Both employees and management in state–owned companies are interested in the maximisation of wages at the expense of profit, although some enterprises are in a better position to pursue this (through price rises, strikes, etc.), than others. State–owned companies are subject, to various degrees, to competition from the private sector and liberalised imports. That is why changes in employment in the various sectors depend mostly on current government policy and decisions concerning import and export constraints, the rate of privatisation, remission of bad credits, etc.

6. The Minimum Wage and Unemployment

Although no precise statistical and econometric analysis has been produced on the effects of the minimum wage on employment, it has been argued that some link exists between an increase in the minimum wage and an increase in unemployment (figure 7.2). We have tried to compare the two sets of figures. It is true that increases in the minimum wage seem to have been followed by corresponding increases in the rate of registered unemployed. This can be observed for instance in February 1991, June 1991, July 1992 and July 1993. Only when the minimum wage in January 1993 slightly increased,

---

[6] This was also one of the conclusions of the ILO–CEET Report, 1993, op. cit.

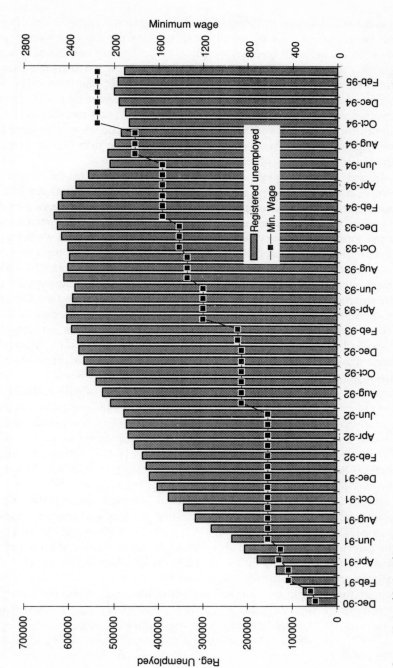

Figure 7.2 *The Minimum Wage and Unemployment, Bulgaria, 1990–95*

Source: National Statistical Institute

was there a decrease in the growth of the registered jobless. This, however, can be explained both by the slight increase of the minimum wage and the seasonal character of unemployment growth. January and February are usually the calmest months in state–owned companies when financial results from the preceding year are awaited before any specific plans are made for the coming year. Besides, in January 1993, in the greater part of state–owned companies, collective bargaining was under way, and there was also a moratorium on lay–offs at this time. In budget–financed enterprises and bodies the beginning of the year is also the time when the new budget is expected and there are usually no enforced redundancies.

In any case, although a minimum wage increase might have a direct effect on unemployment, no statistical analysis of this relationship has yet been carried out. Moreover, we would argue that the existence of such a relationship in Bulgaria has been overemphasised for the following reasons. First, the number of employed receiving the minimum wage has fallen constantly, though sporadically. Second, when studying the relation between the minimum wage and the increase of the number of registered unemployed, we must also take into consideration some peculiarities of the unemployment statistics. The official figures are based on the number of registered unemployed, but many unemployed persons, especially those who do not have the right to receive social benefits, are not listed. The census of 2 December 1992 showed 680,000 unemployed or about 100,000 more than were officially registered at that time. On the other hand, there are a great number of registered unemployed who work in the private sector or in the black economy. According to the official statistics for the period from the first half of 1989 to August 1993, the number of those employed in the state sector decreased by almost 2 million people, that is, by almost half. The number of registered unemployed, however, reached 610,000, which means that 1,400,000 are lost to the statistics. Since 1989 500,000 Bulgarian citizens have emigrated, 350–400,000 of whom were from the working population.

According to the National Statistical Institute the number of those employed in the private sector (including owners and the self–employed) was 242,000 in 1990, 360,000 in 1991, and 470,000 in 1992. In August 1993 the private sector employed about 550–600,000 of those laid off in the public sector. If we add this figure to the number of emigrants, over 1 million people are not statistically accounted for.

It is this enormous number of people that makes the indicator 'registered unemployed' quite useless when trying to determine a cause–and–effect relationship with the minimum wage.

Third, comparison between the rate of the minimum wage and unemployment will not be precise if we do not eliminate seasonal changes. The number of registered unemployed in Bulgaria usually decreases in May and June, when the beginning of the agricultural and tourist season creates many thousands of jobs. At the same time, the number of registered unemployed sharply increases in July because of those graduating from universities and high schools. These peculiarities explain to a great extent the leap in the number of registered unemployed corresponding with the increase of minimum wages. Minimum wages are usually increased in the middle of the year (from 1 July), that is, exactly when graduate students have the right to register and when the minimum wage has become attractive again. It may easily be seen from figure 7.2 that in May and June 1992, with the becoming available of seasonal jobs, the increase in unemployment decreases by three or four times as compared to the previous months, and in July the number of newly registered unemployed grew again considerably, from 5,000 to 30,000 people.

Conscript soldiers, discharged in March or April and in September or October each year, also influence the number of registered unemployed. Unfortunately, the lack of statistics on particular groups according to status at the time of registration does not allow separation of the share of unemployment which may eventually be attributed to the minimum wage increase.

Fourth, the conclusion that the level of the minimum wage and related unemployment benefits encourage people to remain unemployed instead of actively seeking work appears to be too simplistic. In fact, the number of vacancies is symbolic, representing just over 1% of the registered unemployed. These vacancies are available to highly qualified workers who receive wages much higher than the national minimum.

7. The Minimum Wage and Growing Poverty

A change in the level of the minimum wage not only influences wages, it also has a significant effect on impoverishment and social differentiation.

From the beginning of 1992 the National Statistical Institute has estimated the 'minimum living standard', defined as the necessary minimum of goods and services that make possible the physiological existence of the individual. The average level of the minimum living standard is between 60% and 75% of the 'social minimum', which is estimated in parallel with it and takes account of other basic needs. Since the trade unions argue that the official minimum living standard is not sufficient to ensure even the basic subsistence minimum to those receiving it, and that it is the social minimum that should serve as the poverty line, we will compare the minimum wage with both the minimum living standard and the social minimum.

The consumer basket of those living at the level of the 'minimum living standard' is greatly curtailed, as indicated by the fact that foodstuffs only constitute around two–thirds of its volume.

From January 1992 to March 1994 the minimum wage moved from 79.1% to 71% of the minimum living standard (table 7.4). This means that there are many cases in which the whole minimum wage is still not sufficient to cover the minimum food requirements of an employee. The minimum wage also fell below 50% of the social minimum. The uneven change of the ratio between the minimum wage and the minimum living standard (or the social minimum) must also be noted; there are defects in the system for compensating inflation growth.

This question is of exceptional importance and if it is not adequately addressed many thousands of workers may fall below the critical level.

Table 7.4 *Minimum Wage, Minimum Living Standard, and Social Minimum, Bulgaria, 1992–94 (levs)*

Year–month	1 Min. Wage	2 MLS	3 Social Minimum	1/2 (%)	1/3 (%)
Jan–92	620	784	1 234	79.00	50.2
Feb–92	620	830	1 282	74.70	48.3
Mar–92	620	876	1 249	70.78	49.6
Apr–92	620	906	1 290	68.43	48.1
May–92	620	1 001	1 412	61.94	43.9
Jun–92	620	1 035	1 485	59.90	41.7
Jul–92	850	1 015	1 489	83.74	57.0
Aug–92	850	991	1 497	85.77	56.8
Sep–92	850	1 017	1 552	83.58	54.7
Oct–92	850	1 089	1 689	78.05	51.8
Nov–92	850	1 175	1 752	72.34	48.5
Dec–92	850	1 264	1 842	67.25	46.1
Jan–93	890	1 429	1 992	62.28	44.7
Feb–93	890	1 484	2 065	59.97	43.1
Mar–93	1 200	1 585	2 159	75.71	55.6
Apr–93	1 200	1 549	2 095	77.47	57.3
May–93	1 200	1 589	2 155	75.52	55.7
Jun–93	1 200	1 573	2 236	76.29	53.7
Jul–93	1 343	1 553	2 207	86.48	60.8
Aug–93	1 343	1 549	2 278	86.70	58.9
Sep–93	1 343	1 588	2 358	84.57	56.9
Oct–93	1 414	1 661	2 461	85.13	57.4
Nov–93	1 414	1 755	2 604	80.57	54.3
Dec–93	1 414	1 871	2 720	75.57	52.0
Jan–94	1 565	1 950	2 824	80.26	55.4
Feb–94	1 565	2 040	2 954	76.72	53.0
Mar–94	1 565	2 200	3 180	71.14	49.2

Source: National Statistical Institute.

The lagging behind of wages and income due to inflation underlines the overall impoverishment of the population, a key problem for the success of democratic reform.

In the fifth year since the beginning of the changes, not only is the 'man in the street' unable to see any improvement, but his living standards have dramatically fallen.

Unlike the first couple of years, when many people could afford to compensate the fall in their incomes with their savings, sale of property or possessions, cutting back on purchases, etc., most reserves have already been consumed. Any further diminution of personal consumption threatens the very subsistence of large social groups.

The reduction of personal consumption in Bulgaria was 16.1% in 1990, 8.4% in 1991 and 7.4% in 1992. According to preliminary data for 1993, personal consumption is expected to fall by 12%. In other words, over a period of four years, personal consumption in Bulgaria has fallen by approximately 40%.

Bearing in mind income differentials it may be assumed that real personal consumption has fallen by much more than 40% for about one–third of households on the lowest incomes.

Retired people and children are the most vulnerable. The average pension, which is linked to the national minimum wage, represents only one–third of the national average wage, and is so far below the minimum living standard.

The growing trend towards mass impoverishment conceals the threat of social explosion. The other great danger is the establishment of the permanently large property and income differentials characteristic of Latin American countries, circumventing the formation of a significant middle class, which is indispensable for the development of a market economy and a civil society.

Because of this aggravated social situation, bargaining about the minimum wage and low income compensation has become the focal point of social dialogue.

Although collective bargaining has to date played a positive role, considerable joint efforts and compromises on the part of the social partners are needed to call a halt to mass impoverishment and to preserve a significant part of society from almost certain degradation.

8. Conclusion

Under the current economic and social conditions in Bulgaria it is difficult to determine a connection between the minimum wage on one side, and inflation, unemployment and income differentiation on the other.

With regard to the connection between the minimum wage and inflation/ unemployment, this difficulty is due, not only to statistical deficiencies, but above all to underdeveloped market relations and the still relatively important role of administrative decisions in the economy during transition.

For instance, because of the lack of data and methodological problems related to calculation of the unemployment rate, it is difficult to find a definite tendency as regards the relation between the minimum wage and employment or unemployment from the available information and present economic realities in Bulgaria, although a correlation may be discerned between the twofold decrease in the minimum wage over the last four years and the decrease in the number of registered unemployed which started in the spring of 1994, and some equilibration of the labour market. Moreover, the type of relationship between the minimum wage and unemployment can vary between different sectors and enterprises.

The important role of the minimum wage in raising or maintaining people above the minimum living standard cannot be disputed.

The structure of wages and incomes, as well as the share of people living below the minimum living standard, are very much influenced by changes in the level of the minimum wage.

This is why negotiations on the size of the minimum wage are a key issue: whenever the minimum wage is outpaced by inflation the incomes of many people are badly hit, increasing the number of those living below the poverty line. In this respect the development of the minimum wage is rather alarming. Besides being unsteady, the tendency of the minimum wage is very much in a downward direction.

It is evident that the mechanism for determination of the minimum wage now in use should be changed. The main defect of this mechanism (in force from 1 January 1994) is that the size of the minimum wage is corrected to 90% of projected inflation.

The level of the minimum wage has dropped so considerably, however, that for the present 100% compensation for projected inflation will be applied. At the same time, the projective nature of the inflation indicator is of course hypothetical, and often far from economic reality. For the first three months of 1994 real inflation has exceeded its projected level. As a result, in the middle of May the size of the minimum wage was almost half the size of the minimum living standard for one worker. It is three times lower than the average wage, bearing in mind that the difference was 20% in the first half of 1991.

The social partners face a complicated dilemma. On the one hand, they must restore the function of the minimum wage as a bulwark against poverty; that is, its level should be higher than the minimum living standard. On the other hand, the current deep economic crisis makes this difficult. A compromise solution under which the level of the minimum wage is regulated in accordance with the economic realities of transition is the only way forward. A means to overcome discrepancies with regard to the minimum wage is to find another basis for its determination, because the use of different inflation indices has not produced the expected results and led to considerable misunderstandings.

Our proposal is that the minimum wage should be set every three months, subsequent to a rise in the average wage, and at 50% of the average wage over the preceding three months. The average wage is a universal criterion, because it reflects real development in the economy, the labour market and the wage bill. If positive tendencies are present in the economy, the size of the minimum and average wages will increase. Conversely, negative economic tendencies will result in a fall in the average and minimum wages.

Since unemployment among young people is an acute problem it might be worth introducing a special minimum wage for them, set at a percentage (dependent on age) of the national minimum wage.

The problem of the minimum wage and its influence on other economic and social indicators is a difficult and complicated one. The democratic changes in the country and the economy, including tripartite dialogue, must guarantee that an appropriate solution be found in harmony with the interests of employers, employees and society as a whole.

8

The Role of the Minimum Wage in the Romanian Wage Structure

Steliana Pert* and Nicolae Popescu**

1. General Economic Background

Romania is engaged in the wide–ranging, complex and difficult process of transition to a market economy, restructuring and reshaping both economic life and society as a whole. This is a process with no existing theoretical bases or practical solutions, no examples of how to combine different reform measures, or how to divide them into different stages. The fact that the various reform components—legislative, institutional, economic, social, cultural, educational, managerial, behavioural—have different rates of development inevitably leads to breakdowns and failures in the national economy.

The transition to a market economy has proceeded against a general background of profound economic and social crisis. At the same time, the Western industrialised countries are also facing problems related to restructuring and recession. Foreign economic relations have worsened, despite the liberalisation of foreign trade, because of low competitiveness, limited access to Western markets, the abolition of COMECON, and the loss of certain markets in developing countries. Moreover, the embargoes against Iraq and Serbia continue to do serious harm to the Romanian economy when it can least bear it. Lastly, mistakes have been made regarding economic development, reform and its management.

For the last three years of economic reform, Romania has suffered the combined effects of the structural crisis of the centralised economy and economic and social transition (table 8.1). In 1992 GDP was only 68.6% of what it had been in 1989, industrial output 59.7%, and productivity 74.2%. The balance of payments deficit was 6.5% of GDP and the budget deficit 3.6%. The rate of unemployment rose from 3% in 1991 to 10.2% in December 1993. The monthly average inflation rate in 1993 was 12.1% and the exchange rate against the US dollar rose from 30 lei at the end of 1990 to 1,276 lei in December 1993. Last but not least, in December 1993 the consumer price

---

* Romanian Institute of Economics.
** Romanian Ministry of Labour, Wage Department.

Table 8.1 *Macroeconomic Indicators, Romania, 1990–93*

Indicators	1990	1991	1992	1993
Gross Domestic Product				
–billion lei, current prices	857.9	2 198.9	5 982.3	18 835
–1989=100	92.6	79.9	67.9	68.6
Gross Domestic Product				
Per Capita				
–lei, current prices	36 966	98 481	262 508	827 912
–1989=100	91.1	79.1	64.1	64.8
Employed Population				
–thousand persons	10 839.5	10 785.8	10 458.0	10 061.9
–1989=100	99.0	98.5	95.5	91.9
Total Employees				
–thousand persons	8 102.2	7 389.5	6 525.8	6 385.2
–1989=100	101.3	92.4	81.6	79.8
Export FOB, billion lei,				
official exchange rate	135 191	323 693	1 376 092	3 443 088
Import FOB, billion lei,				
official exchange rate	209 912	400 103	1 745 554	3 984 183
Balance of Trade				
–billion lei,				
official exchange rate	–74 721	–76 410	–369 462	–541 095
–% in GDP	9.5	4.0	6.5	2.9
Budget Deficit as				
Percentage of GDP	0.50	1.50	3.60	2.0
official exchange rate				
–lei/USD	23.03	80.08	320.37	760.5
–1989=100	143.90	500.50	2 002.30	4 753.1
Unemployment Rate (%)				
–total	–	3.4	8.4	10.2
–women	–	4.0	10.7	12.6
Average Rate of Inflation (%)	–	10.3	9.6	12.1
Consumer Price Index				
–Oct.1990=100	–	444.5	1 330.0	5 259.9
Index of Average Net Wage				
–Oct.1990=100	–	346.3	955.5	2 967.6
Index of Real Wage				
–Oct.1990=100	–	77.9	71.8	56.4

Source: Monthly Statistical Bulletin; National Commission for Statistics.

index was 5,259% of what it had been in 1989, the net nominal wage 2,968%, while the average real wage represented only 56.4% of its 1990 level.

2. Role and Functions of the Minimum Wage

The problems related to fixing the minimum wage and its development—principles, criteria, function, implementation, etc.—are among the most pressing for government bodies, trade unions and employers' associations. This is partly a result of a process of wage bargaining decentralisation, which has shifted wage determination from the macroeconomic to the microeconomic level. This process involves:

- the dependence of the minimum wage on both economic and social factors. On the one hand, it must cover the vital necessities of the wage earner and his family; on the other, its level and dynamics depend on the overall state of the economy (output, productivity, inflation, etc.);
- the mixed nature of wages: a form of payment (recompense) for work done or services rendered; a cost for the entrepreneur; an income determining the wage earner's expenditure. In these terms the minimum wage expresses a conflict of interest among the social partners, which is particularly difficult to reconcile in an unstable period of transition;
- the minimum wage is a basic element in the structure of wage policies on both the micro– and macroeconomic levels;
- the degree of organisation and the development of bargaining relations between unions and employers;
- the limitations due to a lack of coherence among the various components of reform on prices, taxes, charges, etc;
- the behaviour of the social partners, which has often been adjusted to short–term needs without taking into account the medium– and long–term effects of wage policy.

The main problems are related to the amount of the minimum wage and the leading role that the Government should play in wage determination, while structural imbalances remain and economic indicators continue to decline.

Wage reform, alongside other regulations governing the labour market and the relations between unions and employers, has been a key issue in the transition programme. As a consequence, the minimum wage has been used as a general instrument for wage, income and social security policies.

The institutionalisation of the minimum wage meets several social and economic needs:

- the social protection of those groups of workers most disadvantaged by an unstable labour market;
- micro– and macroeconomic demands springing from the nature of wages and the impact that minimum wage growth might have upon employment, the structure of wages within different sectors, occupational categories, overall wage levels, and inflation.

Before 1989, the wage system was centralised. The minimum wage covered those categorised as unskilled workers or civil servants whose work required no training. Because wages in the previous 'piece rate' system were determined according to certain fixed indicators and a number of other restrictive criteria, very often the actual minimum wage was lower than the one that had been established.

Labour market reform must take into account both wages and social security; the latter, as stipulated in the Constitution and a number of other legal provisions, is indeed a wage–earners' right. The institutionalisation of the national minimum wage, the right to collective bargaining and the obligation to uphold collective agreements are reflected in the Constitution.[1]

According to *Law No. 14/1991, Art. 5 (1)*, 'The national minimum wage is to be established according to the Government's decision after having consulted trade unions and employers' associations'. The minimum wage is fixed for normal working conditions (that is, 170 hours per month); no wages may be lower than the established minimum. The Government may also adjust the minimum wage to changes in the general price index. Table 8.2 presents the evolution of the minimum wage in accordance with government decrees.

The institutionalisation of the minimum wage is one starting point for the many difficult but necessary attitudinal changes of unions and employers towards wages and social protection. As currently conceived, the minimum wage must meet a number of requirements that are difficult to balance:

(a) *Maintaining a minimal living standard* even if the supply of labour exceeds the demand, while not making some workers too expensive for

Table 8.2 *Changes in National Minimum Wage (According to Law No. 14/1991 on Wages), Romania, 1991–94 (lei)*

Period		Gross minimum wage		Gov. Decree No.
		Monthly	Hourly	
1991	March	3 150	18.55	133/1991
	May	5 975	35.15	219/1991
	September	6 775	39.85	579/1991
	November	7 000	41.15	780/1991
1992	January	8 500	50.00	19/1992
	March	9 150	53.80	149/1992
	May	11 200	65.90	218/1992
	September	12 920	76.00	499/1992
	November	15 215	89.50	774/1992
1993	January	16 600	97.65	94/1993
	March	17 600	103.55	124/1993
	May	30 000	176.50	208/1993
	October	40 200	236.45	586/1993
	December	45 000	264.70	683/1993
1994	March	60 000	352.95	90/1994
	July	65 000	382.35	353/1994

Source: Ministry of Labour and Social Protection.

[1] Constitutia Romanei, titlul II, Art. 38 (2) and (5).

employers and keeping to the Government's macroeconomic objectives. The minimum wage should not discourage employment. Trade unions consider the minimum wage insufficient to cover the vital necessities of wage–earners and their families, especially in conditions of rampant inflation. The unions base their argument on the fact that 90% of wage–earners are still working in enterprises that are majority–owned by the state allowing the state to finance the rise of the minimum wage by a reduction in profits. The ratio between the minimum wage fixed by government and the one demanded by the trade unions is 1:2. Although these trade union demands are aimed at protecting the most vulnerable workers, they lead in the state–owned enterprises to a reduction in profits, and it may be argued that this might lead to unemployment, especially when many of the state enterprises are already unprofitable. The private sector could also face problems in coping with minimum wage growth.

(b) The minimum wage is also the *starting point for collective bargaining* in certain sectors, occupational categories and enterprises. Since November 1993, a national minimum wage has been guaranteed for all wage–earners, whether employed in state or privately–owned enterprises. The minimum wage established by collective bargaining is much higher than the national minimum wage in wholly or majority state–owned enterprises, which employ 93% of Romanian wage–earners and 59.3% of the workforce. In those enterprises, the trade unions are quite powerful.

(c) The national minimum wage is the *basic element of all wages* at the microeconomic level, for all wage categories, and for the whole wage structure, since wages at the branch level are adapted according to a coefficient to the national minimum wage. With a strong trade union bargaining position in some sectors this system, however, seems to have created inflationary pressures and led in several enterprises to economic and financial problems. Legislative ambiguities combined with a general managerial crisis have contributed to favour this inflationary behaviour on the part of the social partners, with detrimental medium– and long–term effects.

Romanian legislation does not make a clear distinction between the minimum acceptable wage that is vital for social protection and the basic minimum wage in the wage structure. The latter is established in accordance with the complexity and difficulty of the various work categories. Since wage bargaining is structured on three levels—national, sectoral and enterprise—and the minimum wage accepted at a higher level must be observed lower down, a process of escalation ensues: at the sectoral level the bargained minimum wage rises, exceeding the national minimum wage by 50%, but without being related to economic conditions within

Table 8.3 *Minimum Wage in State–Owned Enterprises (Compared to National Minimum Wage), Romania, 1993 (Index of national minimum wage=1.0)*

	State–owned companies of national importance	State–owned companies of local importance	Total
1.0–1.1	12	25	37
1.1–1.2	4	16	20
1.2–1.3	3	7	10
1.3–1.4	3	6	9
1.4–1.5	3	8	11
1.5–1.6	1	6	7
1.6–1.7	6	4	10
1.7–1.8	2	2	4
1.8	1	5	6
Total	35	79	114

Source: Ministry of Labour and Social Protection. Data from Collective Contracts for 1993 in 114 state–owned enterprises of national or local importance.

the respective sector or enterprise. Table 8.3 also shows how the minimum wage regulations have been influencing wage levels in state–owned enterprises.

As long as imbalances remain between the demand and supply of goods and services, and as long as market mechanisms do not govern wages, the entire wage structure is influenced by rises in low–wage categories and the consequent reaction of higher wages. Besides this, the minimum wage is directly related to other elements of wage and social policy: bonuses for adverse working conditions, pensions, unemployment benefits, social support, etc. For example, unemployment benefit must represent 60–85% of the basic national minimum wage, according to years of service, while allowance for social support represents 40% of the basic national minimum wage; the largest wage supplement for dangerous underground work is as high as the national minimum wage. The numerous compensations and bonuses caused by minimum wage and tariff increases lead to a general growth of nominal wages, irrespective of economic results.

(d) The minimum wage also represents the *main instrument of national wage policy*, enabling structural adjustment of the economy. The amount of the minimum wage and its dynamics are meant to operate directly on the general level and structure of wages, taking into account concrete economic conditions, the labour market, relations between unions and employers and overall economic objectives. By establishing a minimum wage, the Government seeks to reconcile social and economic objectives, and the independent decisions of employers and unions with a view to redressing economic and social imbalances.

3. Size and Development of the Minimum Wage

In 1989, the net minimum wage (representing, in the wage hierarchy, the wage for unskilled work) was 2,000 lei a month, 58.6% of the net average wage. This must be seen against the background of a long–term policy of raising the level of low wages. This minimum wage level was maintained until March 1991, when wage fixing was liberalised. At the same time, the need to fix the minimum wage while reforming the wage system became apparent. In the first governmental decision based on the new wage law, *Decree No. 133/1991*, the gross minimum wage was fixed at 3,150 lei per month, for 170 working hours (18.55 lei/hour). The same decree stipulated the obligation of all natural or legal persons hiring labour to fix wages on the basis of the gross national minimum wage. In March 1991, the new gross national minimum wage represented 59.6% of the gross average wage. In May of the same year, this rose to 64%, because on 1 April a sum of 2,825 lei was added to all wages, the gross minimum wage included, as compensation for price rises.

In the past three years, the minimum wage has been changed 16 times, rising from 3,150 lei a month in March 1991 to 65,000 lei in July 1994, as a result of compensations and additions in accordance with the consumer price index (table 8.2).

Figure 8.1 *Minimum Wage as a Percentage of Average Wage, Romania, 1991–93*

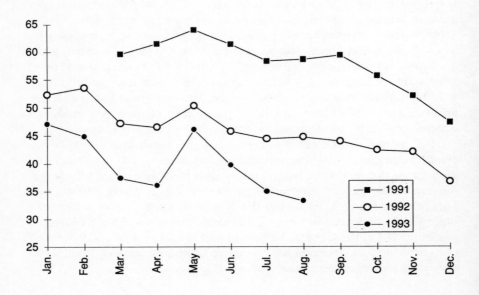

Table 8.4 *Growth of the Gross Minimum Wage and the Gross Average Wage, Romania, 1991–94 (lei)*

		Gross minimum wage	Gross average wage	Minimum wage as % of gross average wage
1991	March	3 150	5 286	59.6
	April	4 675	7 605	61.5
	May	5 975	9 331	64.0
	September	6 775	11 421	59.3
	November	7 000	13 423	52.1
1992	January	8 500	16 241	52.3
	March	9 150	19 373	47.2
	May	11 200	22 258	50.3
	September	12 920	29 415	43.9
	November	15 215	36 152	42.1
1993	January	16 600	35 241	47.1
	March	17 600	47 139	37.3
	May	30 000	65 136	46.0
	September	40 200	102 550	39.2
	December	45 000	131 742	34.2
1994	March	60 000	144 802	41.4
	July	65 000	185 453	35.0

Source: Data released by the Ministry of Labour and Social Security and by the National Commission for Statistics.

Despite the fact that the gross minimum wage in December 1993 was 14 times higher than in May 1991, its proportional relation to the average wage had considerably worsened (figure 8.1 and table 8.4). Whereas in May 1991 the gross minimum wage represented 64% of the average wage, it had fallen to 35% by July 1994. Figures on net minimum and average wages provide a similar picture. The net minimum wage in July 1994 was 37.6%, as compared to 61.3% in March 1991 (table 8.5).

The deterioration of the minimum as compared to the average wage has been caused mainly by the wage formation mechanism. Whereas the national minimum wage rose only with the bonus coefficient established for the whole economy, the average wage rose twice: first by the enterprise bonuses compensating for price rises and then through the annual bargaining round. The relation between the minimum and average wage tends to recover in periods of national compensatory bonuses (for instance, May 1991, 1992, and 1993), but worsens again as a result of collective bargaining. For instance, in May 1993, all wages were supplemented by 10,160 lei, as compensation for the elimination of subsidies. A steady rise in the minimum wage by 70.5% was followed by a general increase of wages, through bargaining, so that the proportional relation between the minimum and average wages dropped again, to as low as 31.3% in September 1993.

Table 8.5 *Net Minimum Wage as Percentage of Net Average Wage, Romania, 1991–94*

	Net average wage							
	Normal tax				20% reduced tax*			
Month	1991	1992	1993	1994	1991	1992	1993	1994
January	–	51.5	47.1	36.7	–	54.3	49.6	–
February	–	52.7	44.8	35.1	–	55.5	47.2	–
March	61.3	47.2	37.3	43.7	64.4	49.8	39.3	–
April	60.2	46.1	36.1	39.0	63.2	48.5	38.1	–
May	62.5	49.8	45.7	38.9	65.8	52.5	48.3	–
June	60.6	45.4	39.5	37.6	63.8	47.8	41.8	–
July	57.1	44.1	37.1	37.6	60.1	46.5	–	–
August	57.3	44.5	33.2	–	60.3	46.9	–	–
September	58.3	43.6	33.3	–	61.4	46.0	–	–
October	54.5	42.2	41.7	–	57.3	44.5	–	–
November	51.4	42.1	35.7	–	54.1	44.4	–	–
December	46.8	36.7	36.6	–	49.3	38.7	–	–

* Since July 1993 a single income tax has been used; the 20% reduced tax which was previously applied to incomes of persons without children was abolished.
Source: Ministry of Labour and Social Protection.

Following rampant inflation, the minimum wage was increased to 40,200 lei on 1 October 1993. As a consequence, the real minimum wage rose by 55.4% compared to March 1991, and the share of the minimum wage in the average wage rose to 36%. Whereas before June 1991 the rate of increase of the minimum wage was higher than the average wage, since that time the reverse has been the case, entailing considerable social difficulties (figures 8.2 and 8.3).

The nature and functions of the minimum wage ought to be clearly separate from those of other wages, and other mechanisms should become operational for social security purposes. Table 8.7 gives details of the fall in the real minimum wage and in the real average wage between 1991 and 1994.

The national minimum wage, which has to take into account existing economic realities and macroeconomic balance, undergoes considerable changes in the process of bargaining, especially at the sectoral level (table

Table 8.6 *Gross Sectoral Negotiated Minimum Wage Compared to National Minimum Wage, Romania, 1992–94*

(Index gross national minimum wage=1.000)

Sector	1992	1993	1994
Ferrous metallurgy	1.040	1.400	1.400
Chemicals and petrochemicals	1.200	1.600	1.600
Mechanical engineering	1.138	1.416	–
Glass and ceramics	1.223	1.562	–

Figure 8.2 *Indices of Net Average Wage, Net Minimum Wage and Consumer Prices, Romania, 1991–94 (Oct. 1990=100)*

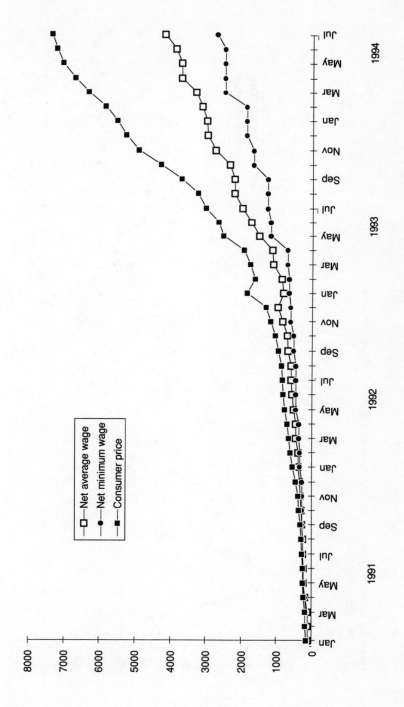

Figure 8.3 *Indices of Real Average Wage and Real Minimum Wage, Romania, 1991–94 (Oct. 1990=100)*

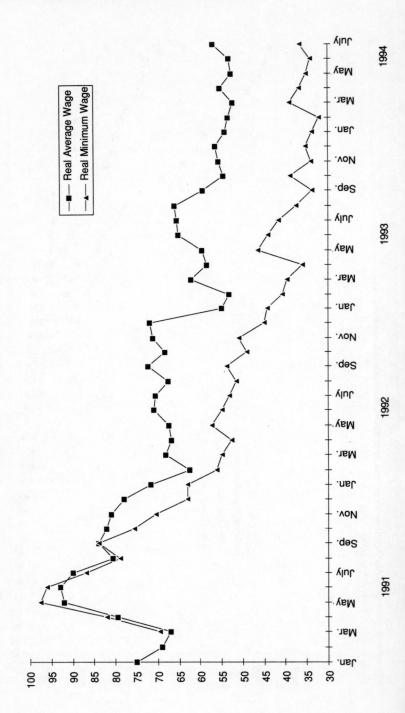

Table 8.7 *Indices of Net Average Wage, Net Minimum Wage, Consumer Prices, Real Average Wage and Real Minimum Wage, Romania, October 1990–July 1994 (October 1990=100)*

		Net average wage	Net minimum wage	Consumer prices	Real average wage	Real minimum wage
1991	January	118.3	–	158.1	74.8	–
	February	116.5	–	169.2	68.9	–
	March	120.4	126.0	180.4	66.7	69.8
	April	182.0	187.2	228.2	79.8	82.0
	May	221.1	235.9	239.8	92.2	98.4
	June	228.1	235.9	244.5	93.3	96.5
	July	241.3	235.9	267.7	90.4	87.8
	August	241.3	235.9	297.6	81.1	79.3
	September	268.7	267.6	319.4	84.1	83.8
	October	287.8	267.6	352.6	81.6	75.9
	November	315.6	277.0	391.0	80.7	70.8
	December	346.3	277.0	444.5	77.9	62.3
1992	January	380.9	334.9	531.2	71.7	63.0
	February	372.5	334.9	597.4	62.4	56.1
	March	447.8	361.1	657.3	68.1	54.9
	April	459.2	361.1	688.0	66.7	52.5
	May	518.7	441.0	771.3	67.3	57.2
	June	569.0	441.0	804.1	70.8	54.8
	July	585.0	441.0	829.6	70.6	53.2
	August	580.1	441.0	857.6	67.6	51.4
	September	682.2	508.6	944.5	72.2	53.8
	October	705.4	508.6	1,035.0	68.2	49.1
	November	833.8	598.8	1,175.0	71.0	51.0
	December	955.5	598.8	1,330.0	71.8	45.0
1993	January	813.1	653.5	1,483.0	54.8	44.1
	February	853.8	653.5	1,605.0	53.2	40.7
	March	1,087.7	692.8	1,752.0	62.1	39.5
	April	1,122.5	692.8	1,927.0	58.3	36.0
	May	1,495.2	1,166.3	2,513.5	59.5	46.4
	June	1,725.5	1,166.3	2,651.1	65.1	44.0
	July	1,963.6	1,245.1	3,000.7	65.4	41.5
	August	2,197.3	1,245.1	3,325.5	66.1	37.5
	September	2,188.5	1,245.1	3,689.1	59.3	33.7
	October	2,335.1	1,661.4	4,291.3	54.4	38.7
	November	2,725.1	1,661.4	4,899.4	55.6	33.9
	December	2,967.6	1,855.1	5,259.9	56.4	35.3
1994	January	2,982.4	1,866.9	5,517.6	54.1	33.8
	February	3,116.6	1,866.9	5,843.1	53.3	32.0
	March	3,300.5	2,462.9	6,328.1	52.2	38.9
	April	3,699.9	2,462.9	6,708.4	55.2	36.7
	May	3,707.3	2,462.9	7,042.4	52.6	35.0
	June	3,844.5	2.462.9	7,233.4	53.2	34.1
	July	4,178.6	2,678.9	7,339.0	56.9	36.5

Source: Calculated on the basis of National Commission of Statistics data.

8.6). The increase of the minimum wage in certain branches, intended to force a general wage rise in those branches, has not always led to the expected results, financial difficulties preventing enterprises from following these sectoral decisions. In such cases, in order to observe this minimum wage, enterprises resorted to a higher rise in low wages. This is also reflected in the higher ratio of the minimum to the average wage in these branches.

For instance, in the chemical industry, the minimum wage has increased to 1.6 times the national minimum wage, whereas in metallurgy the minimum wage has increased to 1.4 times the national minimum wage. As a result, in 1993 the ratio of the minimum wage to the average wage was 45.9% in the chemical industry and 32.8% in metallurgy.

Trade unions have demanded, and sometimes obtained, collective bargaining for a sectoral minimum wage to keep pace with the national minimum wage, so as to obtain a constant ratio between the two. This system for fixing the minimum wage is also to be found in a number of enterprises. This automatic increase in wages and salaries depending on the national minimum wage calls for great care to be exercised when changes in the minimum wage are made. On the macroeconomic level, it may become an inflationary factor, while on the microeconomic level it may discourage employment.

As shown, collective bargaining in some enterprises and branches has led to minimum wages that exceed the national minimum wage. This is the outcome of trade union pressures and the fact that the enterprise owners, in most cases the state, are the beneficiaries of the collective labour contracts. Consequently, they have the same attitude as workers' representatives.

That is why the system of compensation for inflation has aimed at levelling the minimum wages bargained in different enterprises. Each state–owned enterprise has to calculate its own compensation coefficient depending on the sum that represents compensation nationwide, compared to the average wage in the enterprise.

In order to reduce the pressure of wages on prices and to retard inflation, differentiated adjustments of wages to price rises were planned by the Government so as to deter increases in those enterprises where the average wage was much higher than the national average. This mechanism, operative in wholly and majority state–owned enterprises, is based on a system of extra taxes, calculated according to the extent to which the wage fund has been exhausted, incurred when the average wage exceeds the so–called 'average gross calculation wage' fixed for each enterprise. In enterprises with lower average wages, the average gross calculation wage was raised to 86,000 lei for the third quarter of 1993, and 102,245 lei for the fourth. This compensation mechanism, as well as the mechanism adjusting wages to costs, is meant to facilitate wage increases in those enterprises in which most workers receive close to the national minimum wage, while limiting wage increases in the sectors and enterprises where average wages have been too high. In future, when the national minimum wage is fixed, a large number of enterprises will not be affected. At the end of 1993, budget–financed enterprises had also already raised wages above the national minimum average (at the time when it was 45,000 lei per month) to 50,000 lei.

4. Conclusion

The institutionalisation of the minimum wage and its periodic revisions have had various and contradictory effects. From both the economic and the social points of view, the results so far have not met the expectations of the unions or enterprises.

As regards social protection, the primary function of the minimum wage during the transition period, the national minimum wage did not—and still does not—cover the necessities of an employed person. In August 1993, the purchasing power of the net minimum wage had fallen to only 37.5% of its level in October 1990, while that of the average wage had fallen to 66% of its level in October 1990 (figure 8.3).

An analysis of family budgets in 1993 shows that, for families with the lowest wages (with an average number of members of 3.53, and an average number of employed persons of 1.48), income from the basic wage represented only 43% of total expenditure (the average for all the family budgets taken into consideration was 72%). The difference is made up by other sources: allowances for children, unemployment benefits, pensions, own agricultural products, etc.

At the same time, the minimum wage forms the basis for the general system of compensation, which leads to a lack of wage structures in certain branches, for example light industry.

As regards payment of the minimum wage, *Law No. 14/1991* stipulates only the obligation to observe the national minimum wage as a starting point in wage bargaining, without guaranteeing its payment. In these circumstances a number of socially and economically disadvantageous phenomena have appeared against the background of an excess labour force in many enterprises:

– the inability of certain firms to pay negotiated salaries. Thus, there are cases in which wages are lower than the negotiated minimum wage or even the national minimum wage;
– the payment of negotiated wages without careful calculation of its effects on primary costs and prices, thus leading to inflation;
– wage decreases when there is a risk of unemployment.

Law No. 68/1993 (November 1993) guarantees payment of the minimum wage: all persons or companies hiring workers on labour contracts are obliged to ensure payment of a gross wage equal to the gross national minimum wage. The provision is also effective if the employed person is ready to work, but cannot for reasons beyond his control. Although this legislation provides a little more order as regards the minimum wage and greater social stability, on the microeconomic level it ought to have done more as regards labour force rationalisation, particularly in respect of overmanning. On both regional and national levels it may have contributed to raising unemployment.

Three years after the minimum wage was institutionalised, in the present context of economic crisis and declining living standards, two opposite options are often proposed:

- to moderate the minimum wage in order to limit inflationary movements and avoid adverse effects on unemployment; this solution, however, would lower even further the capacity of the minimum wage to provide decent living standards to low–paid workers and to act as an instrument against poverty;
- to increase the minimum wage (by 50–100% of its current level) adapting it regularly to growing inflation and to guarantee low–paid workers' purchasing power in the transition period. However, because of the strong automatic link that seems to prevail in Romania between the national minimum wage and negotiated wages at the sectoral level, this policy might contribute to feeding inflation and to worsening unemployment. This automatic effect of minimum wage increases on wages in different sectors should certainly be limited or abolished in respect of both its social and economic roles.

The only socially and economically acceptable solution seems to lie between these two options. It could only be achieved, however, through a negotiated process and an agreement between government, employers and trade unions, which could ensure the optimal balance between the need for more social protection and the current and evolving economic constraints faced by Romania in its move towards a market economy.

9

The Minimum Wage and Impoverishment in the Republic of Moldova

Valentina Postolachi,* Vasilira Rotaru** and Vassile Stoianov**

1. Introduction

The declaration of sovereignty of the Republic of Moldova, the loss of traditional markets, and the transition to a market economy have set new tasks for the Government, employers and trade unions in respect of wages. New and more flexible forms of ownership have provided a new economic environment in which each employee, irrespective of the sector in which he is employed, has been compelled to revise his attitude to work fundamentally, particularly in respect of remuneration and its components. The minimum wage, its evolution and dynamics, is one of the principle problems in this domain.

Characteristic of the changes which have occurred in wages under the transition to a market economy is the radical transformation of relations between state, enterprises and employees. The *Law on Wages* recently implemented calls for an administrative regime under which only the minimum wage shall be laid down at national level, serving as a social guarantee. Other wage–related issues are the prerogative of enterprises: tariffs and other conditions of remuneration, including its forms and systems, as well as work incentives are established by the enterprise on the basis of bilateral agreements with trade unions or workers' collectives.

2. The Establishment of the Minimum Wage in the Republic of Moldova

In the Republic of Moldova, the minimum wage is enshrined in the *Law on Wages of 25 February 1993,* and serves both as a social guarantee and as a basis for the whole wage structure.

The following are the articles of the Law which deal with the minimum wage:

* Federation of Independent Trade Unions of the Republic of Moldova.
** Centre for Studies of Market Problems, Moldovan Academy of Sciences.

Article 7—The state social guarantees in respect of wages comprise the nationally determined minimum wage, national wage tariffs, state subsidies and benefits.

Article 8—The minimum wage has the character of a social norm and is established on the basis of the minimum consumption budget (minimum subsistence level), representing the acceptable minimum wage paid to the lowest skilled employees.

The minimum wage is subject to revision in accordance with the economic context, the level of labour costs and the average wage, as well as any other relevant changes in the labour market or other socio–economic conditions. The minimum wage is established by government decree after consultation with trade unions and employers.

The minimum wage established in this way is binding on all employers, irrespective of form of ownership, and may not be reduced, either by collective or individual contract.

The national wage tariffs—and those for particular occupational groups—are established on the basis of the minimum wage and tariff coefficients contained in the *Single Tariff Schedule*. They are valid for all workers and take account of qualifications and skills, as well as the quality, importance and complexity of work (table 9.1). The wage tariffs are compulsory and universal in proportion with the available funds.

The national wage tariffs are guaranteed to employees on condition of fulfilment of their work obligations, as defined by collective work contracts (tariff agreements) or individual work contracts.

The national wage tariffs are amended alongside revision of the minimum wage, which is therefore an instrument of macroeconomic policy regulating wage increases and income distribution.

Aiming at the coordination of economic stabilisation measures and the provision of minimum socio–economic guarantees to citizens and the protection of legal rights, a *National Collective Contract* was concluded on 8 July 1994 by the Government, the employers' representatives (the Association of Manufacturers, the Union of Entrepreneurs, and the Federation of Building Employers), and the Federation of Moldovan Independent Trade Unions. It was embodied in *Decree No. 465 of 8 July 1994*. This Contract is considered the basis for the preparation and conclusion of sectoral level collective work contracts with the relevant trade unions. According to the *Law on Collective Work Contracts No.1303–XII of 25 February 1993*, all collective work contracts should be concluded for a definite period, but at least one calendar year.

Collective contracts relate to all employees, regardless of seniority or trade union membership. Equality of treatment is guaranteed regardless of sex, race, nationality, political conviction, membership of any political party, or any other circumstance not related to the skills of the employee.

Table 9.1 *Single Tariff Schedule for Employees in the Budgetary (Public) Sector, Republic of Moldova, 1994*

Wage categories	1	2	3	4	5	6	7	8	9	10	11	12	13	14	15	16	17	18	19	20	21	22	23	24	25	26	27	28	29
Tariff coefficients valid until 1 Jan.1994	1	1.26	1.59	1.81	2.07	2.36	2.69	3.07	3.50	3.85	4.24	4.67	5.14	5.65	6.21	6.83	7.51	8.26	9.09										
Tariff coefficients valid from 1 Jan 1994 to 31 May 1994	1.3 / 1.34	1.67 / 1.3	2.07 / 1.3	2.35 / 1.3	2.70 / 1.3	2.76 / 1.17	3.15 / 1.17	3.59 / 1.17	3.68 / 1.05	4.04 / 1.05	4.45 / 1.05	4.90 / 1.05																	
Tariff coefficients valid after 31 May 1994	2.25 / 2.25	2.58 / 2.05	2.94 / 1.85	3.17 / 1.75	3.31 / 1.60	3.42 / 1.45	3.63 / 1.35	3.84 / 1.25	4.02 / 1.15	4.34 / 1.10	4.45 / 1.05	4.90 / 1.05																	

The coefficients in the denominator increase the tariff coefficients within the Single Tariff Schedule, as obtained in accordance with the *Law on Wages of 25 February 1993.*

Collective work contracts are concluded at three levels: national, sectoral and enterprise. Employees are represented by their trade union during the conclusion of these collective contracts.

In accordance with their statutes, the trade unions participate in negotiations regarding the minimum wage, as well as many questions of a socio–economic character included in the *National Collective Contract* through the *National Mediation Committee for Collective Negotiations*. The National Mediation Committee was created in conformity with the *Law on Collective Work Contracts*. It is a permanent body comprising an equal number of representatives of the Government, trade union organisations recognised at national level and employers' organisations.

The activities of the Committee are based on the Constitution, the *Law on Collective Work Contracts*, and other normative acts, standards of international law valid on the territory of the Republic of Moldova, Decrees of the President of the Republic of Moldova and regulations of the National Mediation Committee for Collective Negotiations.

The regulations on the minimum wage in Moldova were introduced in a period of increasing inflation. The *Law on the Indexation of Incomes of 24 December 1991* was adopted at the same time.

The indexation procedure is as follows:

– part of the wage, equivalent to a maximum of twice the national minimum monthly wage, is indexed at 50% of any rise in the CPI;
– the remainder of the wage, equivalent to a maximum of the national minimum monthly wage, is also indexed at 50% of any rise in the CPI.

This means that no income higher than three times the national minimum monthly wage is indexed. Enterprises may allocate additional funds to cover wage indexation from their own resources, if required by a collective work contract, up to a limit of five times the consumer price index. The *Law on the Indexation of Incomes* has not, however, been implemented due to continuing economic difficulties.

Since the adoption of the *Law on Wages of February 1993* the minimum wage has been revised only four times (table 9.2). Article 15 of the Law stipulating that wages should follow price increases has not been followed and the trade unions have complained that the minimum wage has fallen well below the subsistence minimum (figure 9.1).

3. Economic Functions of the Minimum Wage

From March 1993, the minimum wage became an instrument of macroeconomic policy, used (by means of Presidential Decree and decrees related

Table 9.2 *Changes in Legislation on the Minimum Wage, Republic of Moldova, 1986–94*

Date	Minimum Wage		Legislation		
	Roubles	USD*			
Until 01.91	80	141	Government Decree	No. 1115	17.09.86
01.01.91	100	176	Government Decree	No. 73	12.02.91
01.04.91	165	290	Government Decree	No. 143	22.03.91
01.01.92	400	3.64	Presidential Decree	No. 755	27.12.91
01.04.92	850	8.50	Presidential Decree	No. 81	04.04.92
01.07.92	1,700	4.01	Presidential Decree	No. 15	15.07.92
01.03.93	3,000	4.55	Presidential Decree	No. 28	25.02.93
01.07.93	7,500	7.28	Presidential Decree	No. 91	21.06.93
	Leu	USD			
01.11.93	10.0	2.92	Presidential Decree	No. 182	01.10.93
01.01.94	13.5	3.69	Presidential Decree	No. 228	24.12.93
01.06.94	18.0	4.46	Presidential Decree	No. 181	31.05.94

* High USD figures in 1991 reflect an exchange rate kept at an artificially very low level.

to the *Single Tariff Schedule*) to influence the general level and structure of wages, aiming at the solution of considerable national problems: regulation of economic activity, optimisation of income distribution, and social protection for the needy. The minimum wage thus became decisive in

Figure 9.1 *The Dynamics of Living Standards Indices in the Republic of Moldova (1992 to the 1st half of 1994–in $)*

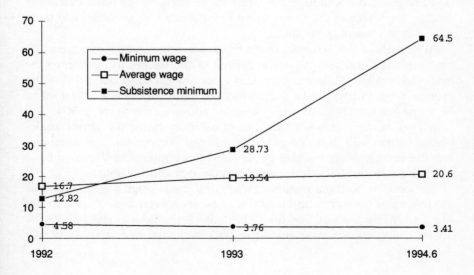

Table 9.3 *Minimum Wage and Average Wage, Republic of Moldova, 1991–94*

	1991	1992	1993	1994 (first half)
Minimum wage	148.80	879.20	5 450	13.50
Minimum wage USD*	261.90	4.58	3.76	3.41
Average wage	434	3 477	30 000	81.90
Average wage USD*	764.10	16.7	19.54	20.68
Minimum wage/ Average wage	0.34	0.25	0.19	0.16

The indices for 1991 to 1993 are given in roubles, and for 1994 in leu.
* High USD figures in 1991 reflect an exchange rate kept at an artificially very low level.

the determination of remuneration for a considerable portion of working people.

The minimum wage tariffs have both a direct and an indirect impact on actual wages. The direct impact is due to the linkage between the minimum wage and other wage tariffs (on the basis of the coefficients of the *Single Tariff Schedule*). The indirect impact is a result of institutional mechanisms: if a wage is established by collective negotiation on the basis of minimum wage tariffs, it is more or less automatically corrected in line with any increase of the minimum wage.

The minimum wage determined in this manner provides an instrument of income redistribution and so a concrete means to harmonise the wages of different categories of worker. But a whole series of complex problems must be overcome before the redistributive role of the minimum wage can be fully realised. Although the need for centralised decision–making is evident, the ability of the Government to influence entrepreneurs and trade unions is at present quite limited.

An analysis of the dynamics of the minimum wage and the average wage between 1991 and 1994 shows a decline of the former in relation to the latter (table 9.3). While the minimum wage amounted to one–third of the average wage in 1991, and a quarter in 1992, in the first half of 1994 it fell to only one–sixth or 16%. In the developed countries the figure is 50%.

In view of the increase in the rate of inflation during the period under consideration, and in order to obtain a better comparison, the minimum and the average wage (as well as the subsistence minimum shown in table 9.5) are presented in both the national currency and US dollars.

The trend of both the minimum wage and the average wage, as well as the minimum consumption budget, may be seen even more clearly in figure 9.1. While the fact that up to 1991 the Republic was still part of the Soviet Union, which maintained the USD exchange rate at an artificially

Table 9.4 Average Monthly Wage of Employees in 15 Sectors of the National Economy, Republic of Moldova, 1991–94

	1991		1992		1993		1994 (months 1–6)	
	Average monthly wage (roubles)	% of the national average wage	Average monthly wage (roubles)	% of the national average wage	Average monthly wage (leu)	% of the national average wage	Average monthly wage (leu)	% of the national average wage
Total	401.5	100.0	3 477	100.0	30.0	100.0	81.9	100.0
Industry	460.2	114.6	4 559	132.2	42.9	143.0	127.3	155.4
Agriculture	432.9	107.8	3 269	93.9	24.6	82.0	52.1	63.6
Forestry	211.0	52.6	2 515	72.3	28.3	96.0	75.3	91.9
Building	444.5	110.7	3 791	109.0	35.7	119.0	131.8	160.9
Transport	402.5	100.2	3 491	100.4	30.7	102.3	104.7	127.8
Utilities and social services	335.8	83.6	3 699	106.3	32.4	113.3	118.9	145.2
Telecommunications	375.7	93.6	3 379	97.2	28.0	93.3	112.4	137.2
Trade and catering	362.4	90.3	2 706	77.8	27.7	92.3	87.4	106.7
Health care	344.1	85.7	2 687	77.2	27.6	92.0	83.1	101.5
Education	295.8	73.7	2 931	84.2	25.5	85.0	72.8	88.9
Science and scientific services	453.4	112.9	3 267	94.0	32.2	107.3	115.6	141.1
Finance	806.9	201.0	7 734	222.4	97.5	325.0	233.9	285.6
Management organisations	408.0	101.6	4 302	123.7	36.7	122.3	119.7	146.2
Informatics and computer services	376.0	93.6	2 684	77.2	26.2	87.3	107.9	131.7
The arts	255.6	63.7	3 087	88.8	26.0	86.7	74.2	90.6

low level, must be taken into account, living standards at that time were much higher than today.

The application of the *Single Tariff Schedule* to public employees also influenced the level of the average wage, removing some distortions and generating others. The national average wage for 1993 was 8.8 times higher than the previous year and amounted to 30,000 roubles. Although the public sector was not entirely left behind (health care remuneration was up 10.2 times compared to 1992, science and scientific services 10 times, and administrative staff 9.2 times), the situation of other public employees was not so fortunate, compounded by delays in the payment of wages. Employees of private enterprises, although often with lower qualifications, did rather better. The different economic possibilities of enterprises and the lack of wage regulation by the state resulted in a further increase of wage differentials, the situation of employees in the public sector being the worst. As shown in table 9.4 in 1991 employees in education, health care, and the arts were ranked 13th, 11th and 14th respectively out of 15 sectors of the national economy, and 12th, 11th and 10th in 1992. A comparative analysis of wage dynamics shows that, following the introduction of the *Single Tariff Schedule* in 1994, wage differentiation has decreased; thus, wages in education increased (as regards the national average) from 73.7% in 1991 to 88.9% in 1993, in health care from 85.7% to 101.5%, and in the arts from 63.7% to 90.6% (table 9.4).

In order to regulate the wages of employees in all sectors of the national economy, a mechanism is needed to restrict unjustified wage increases in the private sector and correspondingly to bring wage levels in the public sector up to a more equitable level. When establishing the possible tariff rates for basic occupations in the first wage category, the trade unions, the employers and the Government should endeavour to avoid placing too great a burden on employers, and to establish a minimum wage structure which would ensure a minimum guarantee for low paid workers and so entice people to take low paying jobs rather than remain dependent upon benefits. It should also reduce wage differentials in sectors of the national economy which reflect neither results, quality nor other performance factors.

Deviation from the principle of comparable pay for comparable work, irrespective of sector or form of ownership, is likely to generate social tensions. The *Single Tariff Schedule* makes it possible to take all the relevant factors into account, while public sector employers may, whenever necessary, boost their employees' incomes by such means as bonus payments.

A condition for accomplishing this aim, as well as for the short–term maintenance of the *Single Tariff Schedule* (its amendments and supplements of

1993 included), is a considerable increase in budgetary allocations for the payment of wages: these allocations, consisting of bonus payments and indexations, are meant to compensate and stimulate the workforce.

4. The Minimum Wage: An Instrument of Social Protection?

In the course of the Republic of Moldova's transition to a market economy a conspicuous gap between rich and poor has become increasingly evident.

A 'nouveau riche' stratum has made its appearance, largely the owners and higher management of banks, joint ventures, trading companies, and of course the more illicit corners of the business world. In this category, those receiving their salaries and other income (at least partly) in convertible foreign currencies (USD, DM, etc.) are particularly favoured.

Given a USD exchange rate of the Moldovan leu of 3.8 to 4.2 leu to the dollar between December 1993 and March 1994, the average wage of as little as 30 leu a month provides the majority of the population with wages of below 10 dollars. This index is even lower than in developing countries and reflects the deplorably low levels of investment in Moldova. Moreover, under conditions of a rapid increase in the prices of various goods and services, real wages have fallen dramatically, putting the majority of workers into poverty (figure 9.2).

Clearly, the economic situation is getting worse and worse, and it will be almost impossible to slow down the decline in living standards in the

Figure 9.2 *Minimum Wage and Average Wage Compared to Subsistence Minimum, Republic of Moldova, 1991–94*

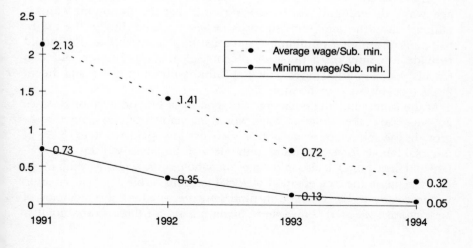

Table 9.5 *Minimum Wage and Subsistence Minimum, Republic of Moldova, 1991–94*

	1991	1992	1993	1994 (first half)
Minimum wage	148.80	879.20	5 450	13.50
Minimum wage USD*	261.90	4.58	3.76	3.41
Minimum subsistence level	203.8	2 463.20	41 600	255.50
Minimum subsistence level USD*	358.6	12.82	28.73	64.50
Minimum wage/ Minimum subsistence	0.73	0.36	0.13	0.05

The indices for 1991 to 1993 are given in roubles, and for 1994 in leu.
* High USD figures in 1991 reflect an exchange rate kept at an artificially very low level.

foreseeable future. The need to provide at least reasonable material conditions by increasing wages is not, however, dictated only by humanitarian concerns, but equally by economic exigencies: only in this way can workers be expected to adopt the kind of attitude required by a market economy.

Minimum social guarantees should provide a subsistence income to all, which it clearly failed to do in 1993–1994, but the minimum wage established on 1 January 1993—equivalent to 3,000 roubles—represented only 12.5% of the minimum consumption budget in January 1994, the subsequent minimum wage rate of 13.5 leu only 7%, and that of 18 leu established on 1 June 1994 only 5%. These dramatic developments of the minimum wage and the minimum subsistence level are presented in table 9.5.

On the basis of tables 9.3 and 9.5 and figure 9.2, it is obvious that average wage differentials are increasing, and that the minimum wage is falling below the minimum subsistence level. Accordingly, the establishment of a higher minimum wage must be considered, and it should provide not only for a person's physiological requirements, but also for his socio–cultural ones, since spiritual wellbeing has a significant impact on physical wellbeing.

At the same time, the economic situation must be borne in mind, since any increase in the minimum wage would inevitably result in general wage growth: the minimum wage not only covers low–paid workers (5.7% of the total labour force according to the data of the Ministry of Labour, Welfare and the Family), it also influences the whole wage scale. Any fall might easily result in the exacerbation of social tensions. This negative situation is particularly to be observed in rural settlements where the members of agricultural collective farms often remain unpaid for three to six months.

In order further to assist the more vulnerable layers of society and in compliance with the Presidential Decree on the minimum wage and additional measures of social protection of 29 December 1993 and 31 May 1994, new coefficients have been included in the *Single Tariff Schedule*, making possible a wage increase for certain categories of employee in the manufacturing and budgetary spheres (table 9.1). Accordingly, the wages of employees of category 1 (the lowest) were increased by 1.3 times from 1 January 1994, and by 2.25 times from 1 June 1994 in respect of the minimum wage. In accordance with these Decrees, all categories of pensions have also been increased.

Although no official statistical data are available, many enterprises fail to pay wages on time. The amount of unpaid wages increased by 8.3 million leu between 1 May and 1 June this year, reaching a total of 83.4 million leu. Seventy two per cent of this sum represents the outstanding wages of agricultural employees.

The difficult economic and financial circumstances continue to have a negative impact on living standards. Between January and May 1994, the income of the population fell by 65% in comparison with the consumer price index.

5. Conclusion

The state has a duty to provide a minimum level of income for all persons, using all legislative and fiscal means at its disposal. Current minimum wage policy is, however, inadequate, both from an economic and a social viewpoint, since the level of the minimum wage represents only 5% of the minimum subsistence level (minimum consumption budget). Not only are unskilled workers living below the poverty line, but well–qualified occupational groups are also hard hit: although the national average wage is currently five times the minimum wage, more than 80% of the average wage goes on food. Average wages also fell well below the poverty line.

On the economic level, this policy appears to be inadequate to motivate the labour force to work harder or to acquire more skills and qualifications. Moreover, this strict control of the minimum wage is based on the assumption that any increase in the minimum wage would have a direct effect on the average wage in the economy, which does not seem to be proven in reality. And even if this was the case, the social partners could try to control wage increases in the whole economy without central controls, by collective bargaining and the conclusion of collective agreements, not only at the national level, but also at the sectoral and enterprise levels. At the same time, the very strict *Single Tariff Schedule* not only leads to excessive rigidity in the wage determination process, it also leads to excessive and artificial wage differentiation between categories of workers, wages in the highest category (the 29th) being 20 times higher than in the lowest category. In this respect, the *Tariff Schedule*, which includes 22 categories, and in which the wages of employees in the 22nd category are only 6 times higher than those of employees in the first, would definitely be better.

More freedom should also be given to additional forms of remuneration, which could be negotiated between the social partners, and fixed in accordance with the situation, but also budgetary constraints. In the context of the Moldovan economy, where the situation does not seem to allow the fulfilment of trade union demands for a minimum wage level equivalent to the subsistence minimum, it is crucial that the social partners be allowed to adapt the minimum wage and the average wage to economic conditions, whether at the national, the sectoral or the enterprise level. Only in this more decentralised way could the Government have some chance of halting the continuous fall of the minimum wage relative to the subsistence minimum, and avoid a further deterioration of the social climate.

10

Minimum Wage Protection in Western Industrialised Economies

Stephen Bazen* and Gilbert Benhayoun**

1. Introduction

Systematic legal minimum wage fixing has existed for over a century in capitalist economies. The aim of the first minimum wage systems of New Zealand, Australia and Great Britain was to provide protection for workers in a minority of sectors where exploitation was rife. Over time minimum wage fixing has come to be present in the vast majority of capitalist economies for different reasons and in various forms. Current practice has recently been influenced by the combined impact of high unemployment and the return to dominance of neoclassical economics. However, the dilution of the protection afforded by minimum wage fixing is only justifiable if it can be shown to have had discernibly detrimental effects: empirical evidence seems to suggest that recourse to the simplistic labour market models which have often dominated neoclassical economic analysis of the impact of minimum wages is not justified. In the first section we present three approaches to minimum wage fixing that are found in Western capitalist countries. We go on to examine the economic impact of minimum wages in the second section by reviewing the underlying theoretical reasoning, pointing out the difficulties encountered when attempting to identify the impact of minimum wages on employment and the wage structure, and briefly surveying the studies that have been undertaken of the US and European experience. The conclusion that emerges is that in some countries there are doubts concerning the existence of an effect on employment, and where an impact is found the size of the effect is small and confined to young persons. In the final section some implications are drawn for minimum wage fixing in Central and Eastern Europe.

2. Forms of Minimum Wage Protection

The form that minimum wage fixing takes determines its effectiveness in protecting vulnerable workers as well as its economic impact. The notion of

* IERSO, Université de Bordeaux I.
** CER, Université d'Aix–Marseille III.

a minimum wage is usually presented as a statutory, imposed and more often than not, a single, universally applicable, national minimum wage rate. These notions, however, are abstractions as all minimum wage systems contain exceptions, as well as variations in the minimum rates applicable and in the majority of the OECD countries there is no statutory national minimum wage.

Most workers in most capitalist economies have their basic wages determined through collective bargaining. Collective agreements usually fix minimum rates for different types of employee. In this sense collective agreements provide minimum wage protection for the employees they cover.

However, rates differ from sector to sector and increasingly from enterprise to enterprise. Overlaid on this system there are often legal minimum wage rates that must be respected at least in some sectors, and certain groups of workers are left unprotected due to the absence of collective bargaining and legal minimum wages in the sectors where they work.

Three examples serve to illustrate the different approaches. The most complete form of minimum wage protection is to be found in France. The national minimum wage—the SMIC—applies to all workers aged 18 and over with lower, but legally binding, minimum rates for workers aged under 18, apprentices and handicapped workers. The SMIC is uprated at least once a year and is linked to the consumer price index and average wages. In addition there are nationally negotiated branch agreements which fix a structure of minimum rates and these are legally binding on all enterprises in a given branch. Furthermore the social partners are legally obliged to enter into wage negotiations. The consequence of this approach is a highly regulated wage structure with a high degree of minimum wage protection for all employees. Labour inspectors are charged with enforcing all legal minimum wage rates whether determined by statute or through collective bargaining. Around 10% of employees receive the SMIC which is fixed at around 60% of the median wage.

In the United States there is a national (federal) minimum wage supplemented by state minimum wage laws. The national minimum wage is legally binding on employers but applies to only some 85% of the labour force. The main categories of worker excluded are outside workers such as sales representatives, supervisory staff and certain types of agricultural worker. It is indexed on neither prices nor average wages and is uprated by Congress at irregular intervals. State minimum wage rates appear in general to be uprated more regularly than the national minimum and apply in some states to certain groups of worker not covered by the federal minimum. Collective bargaining is not the major method of wage determination since only 30% of workers are covered by collective agreements and many rates are determined on an individual basis. Such a minimum wage system leaves some workers unprotected and wages in sectors not covered may be pushed down by the minimum wage in the sectors which are. Furthermore, there is strong evidence of noncompliance by some enterprises in the covered sectors. Due to the irregularity in its uprating (its value as a proportion of average manufacturing earnings fell from 40% to 32% between 1981 and 1989) the numbers receiving the national minimum wage vary. At its 1981 peak it affected about 12% of employees compared to only 3% in 1988.

In Great Britain there is no longer any statutory minimum wage fixing. However, from 1909 to 1993 the Trade Boards and then the Wages Councils set statutory minimum wage rates for certain sectors which although relatively large in number (there were twenty six at the end of their existence) employed less than 15% of the workforce. The rates established varied since each sector had its own Wages Council which each year independently fixed minimum wage rates through a form of collective bargaining with independent members arbitrating when no agreement could be reached. Relative to average earnings in the British economy, the minimum rates were set at around 35% to 40%. Noncompliance was a key feature of the system due to the complexity of the wage structures set (although these were simplified after 1988), and the inadequate resources devoted to enforcement.

In addition to these combinations of statutory and collective approaches to minimum wage fixing, in some countries the sole form of protection is through collectively agreed minimum rates (Germany, Italy and Denmark for example), which has the advantage that wage rates are established by agreement rather than through legal imposition. To the extent that the collective bargaining process incorporates prevailing economic conditions minimum rates can be set in a less arbitrary manner than in statutory systems with rigid indexation mechanisms. On the other hand, collective bargaining does not cover all groups of workers, and because of the recent trend towards decentralisation the advantages of national branch or occupational level agreements have been undermined. That is, while centralised bargaining provides effective minimum wage protection and takes into account prevailing conditions at the national level, decentralised bargaining brings wage determination closer to the level of the enterprise where asymmetries in bargaining power will in certain cases undermine minimum wage protection and distance wage fixing from national economic conditions.

3. The Economic Impact of Minimum Wages

(a) The Issue

As stated above, the form taken by minimum wage fixing determines to some extent the economic impact of minimum wages. A minimum wage that affects only 3% of the labour force will have a different impact from one that affects 20%. Furthermore, if employment is reduced in sectors where minimum wages apply, the existence of non–covered sectors in which wages are flexible downwards may absorb some of the employment effect.[1] A national minimum wage will leave some enterprises totally unaffected and make survival difficult for others. In order to put the economic impact of minimum wages in perspective, it is first necessary to appreciate their role and how they are seen by enterprises.

The notion of a minimum wage implies that without it at least some wage rates would be lower. In a buoyant, fully–employed economy minimum wages would be redundant as enterprises would have to bid up wages in order to satisfy their labour requirements. The argument for minimum wages lies in the existence of groups of workers whose labour is not sufficiently scarce relative to demand. In such circumstances enterprises have the upper hand and can continue to force down wages as long as there are workers still seeking employment.

The role of minimum wages is to prevent enterprises from acting in this manner, protecting those not covered by collective bargaining arrangements. Enterprises are unable to enhance their profits or improve their competitiveness by driving down the lowest wage rates.

Whether the existence of minimum wages results in lower employment levels depends on various factors. Where enterprises can only produce and sell profitably if wages are lower than the minimum wage some employment effects are inevitable. The issue that must then be addressed is whether enterprises, as job creators, should be allowed to pay the lowest wages they can, or whether at the cost of certain activities being rendered unprofitable, the most vulnerable employees should be afforded protection. Where enterprises can pay higher wages in the absence of minimum wage protection, there will clearly be no reduction in employment so long as the minimum wage is set at a reasonable level. In general, the higher the minimum wage the greater the risk of employment being reduced.

Once in place, minimum wage rate increases will also result in reductions in employment if enterprises seek to replace low wage labour with capital or if competitiveness is reduced. It is not uncommon for increases in minimum wages to be absorbed by enterprises passing on the higher cost to consumers, or by reducing profits or adjusting the non–wage elements of labour costs. There is also the possibility of a 'shock' effect whereby increases in minimum wage rates provoke enterprises to improve their organisation by tightening up procedures and raising productivity. There is no automatic tendency for increases in minimum wages to reduce employment. Indeed, in the single buyer or monopsony situation minimum

---

[1] G. Fields: 'The unemployment effects of minimum wages', in *International Journal of Manpower*, 15, 1994, pp. 74–81.

wages can actually lead to increased employment. This occurs if enterprises find that they can prevent profits being eroded (as a result of increased labour costs) by expanding output.

As unemployment rose to record levels in the OECD countries, with particularly high rates experienced by groups likely to be paid at or near the minimum wage (such as young persons and unskilled workers), minimum wage fixing was increasingly called into question. Keynesian macroeconomic policies which had failed to bring down unemployment during the period of high inflation at the end of the 1970s were increasingly being abandoned and attention concentrated more on the supply side as the reason for high and persistent unemployment. The functioning of the labour market—in particular wage inflexibility—was seen by many as a significant element both in rising unemployment and the difficulties encountered in trying to bring it down quickly. This change of emphasis in policymaking led minimum wage fixing to be identified as a possible major cause of unemployment.

In several countries minimum wage protection was diluted during the 1980s. The US federal minimum wage was frozen throughout the Reagan presidency (1981 to 1989) at USD3.35 an hour. In the Netherlands the national minimum wage was frozen from 1984 to 1989 and the sub–minimum rates for young persons were reduced.

In Great Britain, persons under the age of 21 were removed from the scope of the Wages Councils' minimum wage rates (which had previously applied, albeit at reduced rates, to all workers aged 16 or over). In France, when the Socialist government was replaced by a right wing coalition in 1986, the minimum wage was uprated strictly in line with indexation requirements and no more, leading to a fall in its value relative to average earnings. In each case the impact of minimum wages on employment was cited as the reason for diluting minimum wage protection.

(b) The Evidence

In view of the political response to the notion that minimum wage fixing leads to falling employment, and given that in principle employment can be reduced, increased or left unaltered by minimum wage fixing, it is essential to examine the issue empirically. There are essentially two questions to be answered:

– What is the direction of the effect of minimum wages on employment?
– How large is the impact?

Clearly these questions can be refined by examining who is affected most (for example, young persons or adults) and whether the effects are stable over time or in relation to certain circumstances. In addressing these questions various intermediate stages in the passage from the theoretical basis of the relationship between employment and minimum wages to its empirical testing have to be clarified.

(i) Theoretical Considerations

The standard neoclassical model is specified for a sector in terms of enterprise demand for a given, homogeneous type of labour as a function of the marginal cost of labour and its supply in terms of the wage. Where supply and demand are equal the wage is the equilibrium wage. In these circumstances a minimum wage fixed above the equilibrium wage reduces demand for labour and increases its supply (if the curve has the conventional upward slope) so that employment is reduced and unemployment created in excess of the number made redundant. This theoretical approach is less informative regarding the extent of the impact. Marshall and later Hicks showed that, under certain conditions, the elasticity of labour demand with respect to the wage is higher in absolute terms in sectors where the elasticity of product demand with respect to price, the elasticity of substitution between labour and other factors, the proportion of labour costs in total costs and the elasticity of supply of other factors are all high.[2] This would indicate that minimum wages would have the largest impact in sectors where wages were low, production was labour intensive but easily made more capital intensive, and where product markets were competitive.

In the case of an effective minimum wage (that is, one established above the equilibrium wage and fully complied with) the standard approach is unambiguous on the direction of the impact on employment within the sector in question. If other sectors are not covered by minimum wage fixing arrangements those displaced may be absorbed elsewhere at a wage lower than the minimum.

This situation would be relevant to the British Wages Councils and the US federal minimum wage in formal terms but applicable to any system if the non–covered sector is the informal or black economy. Thus the impact on employment depends on the coverage of the minimum wage fixing arrangements and on the size of the informal sector. The extent to which the latter absorbs workers displaced by the formal, covered sectors is, of course, extremely difficult to observe.

Another issue is the empirical difficulty of identifying homogeneous groups of workers. Within a sector there will be several types of worker and a whole set of wage rates. Even within the unskilled category there is a wide variation in wages. The effect of the minimum wage on the employment of such a group is therefore not the same as that identified in

---

[2] Hicks: *The Theory of Wages* (London, Macmillan, 1932).

theoretical terms. The impact on employment is more complicated for two reasons. First, effective minimum wages initially compress the lower end of the wage distribution. Among the lowest paid differentials are reduced and in some cases eliminated. If employers and (organised) workers strive to maintain wage differentials in order to reward effort, responsibility and seniority, minimum wages (and increases thereof) will entail knock–on or ripple effects through the lower part of the wage structure. The impact on labour costs is not confined to an increase in the wages of those directly affected. The second complication arises due to the heterogeneity of the group of workers considered and the possibilities of substitution between different types of worker within the same group. If minimum wages entail a substitution effect between different types of worker within the same group, the overall effect on the group's employment will be negligible.

The difficulty of empirically identifying minimum wage workers as a homogeneous group has meant that most studies have examined the impact on the employment of groups or sectors which contain large proportions of minimum wage workers. In fact, the vast majority of empirical studies examine the impact of minimum wages on the employment of young persons. The latter are normally aged 25 or under and typically represent between 30 and 40% of those receiving the minimum wage. Having said that, while young persons, lacking experience and on–the–job training, often start out on low wages they then move up the ladder. Where minimum wage fixing arrangements are in place it is normal that a large proportion of young persons receive the minimum wage. It must not be overlooked, however, that women workers (young and adult together) consistently make up about two–thirds of the minimum wage population.

(ii) Estimation Issues

Most empirical work in this field uses time series data (unless there are different minimum rates set sectorally or by region there is insufficient variation in the minimum wage to identify its impact on employment from cross section data.). However, over time many variables move simultaneously and it is difficult to disentangle the effects of each variable. Econometric methods enable the estimation of the relevant parameters only if the model is clearly specified: all the relevant, systematic influences on employment must be incorporated in the estimation process. Furthermore, it is important to take into account the dynamic aspects of the relationship between employment and minimum wages since some important effects can take time to emerge or to run their course.

Examples of this last point are very revealing. For example, Brown, Gilroy and Kohen examined the employment–minimum wage relationship for teenagers in the US using time series data.[3] Their static model revealed that minimum wage increases had reduced teenage employment by about 1% for a 10% increase in the minimum wage. A test of the statistical significance of the result confirmed its existence. However, when 'dynamic' aspects of the relationship were introduced the effect was not statistically significant. It took a subsequent article by Solon to 'restore' the initial result by respecifying the dynamic process involved,[4] and the latest work using US time series data suggests that the effect is even smaller.[5]

A similar sequence occurred in studies of the French experience. Rosa found in a similar model to that of Brown et al. that the minimum wage in France had reduced the employment of young persons in a statistically significant fashion.[6] However, when Martin reexamined the issue taking into account the fact that such employment was highly trended, there was no statistically significant effect attributable to the minimum wage.[7] Again, later studies do find that minimum wages have an effect on young persons' employment (see below).

(iii) The US Experience: Two Generations of Studies?

The vast majority of studies of the impact of minimum wages on employment have examined the US experience. In their survey of studies undertaken up to 1980 Brown, Gilroy and Kohen found that a 10% rise in the federal minimum wage reduced teenagers' employment by between 1 and 3%.[8] They argued that the lower end of the range was most significant. They also found that there was little or no effect on adult employment. However, in order to identify reasons for the divergent results in different studies, they undertook their own analysis of a common data set and examined how changes in model specification altered the results. They found that the lower bound of the range was indeed the more reliable estimate, but also, as has already been pointed out, that the dynamic aspects of the relationship render the minimum wage effect insignificant. Follow–up work reaffirmed the existence of an effect, albeit a smaller one.[9]

[3] C. Brown, C. Gilroy and B. Kohen: 'Time series evidence of the effect of minimum wages on youth employment and unemployment,' in *Journal of Human Resources*, 18, 1983, pp. 3–31.

[4] G. Solon: 'The minimum wage and teenage employment.: the role of serial correlation and seasonality,' in *Journal of Human Resources*, 20, 1985, pp. 292–97.

[5] A. Wellington: 'The Effect of the Minimum Wage on Youth Employment; An Update,' in *Journal of Human Resources*, 26, 1991, pp. 27–46.

[6] J. J. Rosa: The effect of minimum wage regulation in France in S. Rottenberg (ed.): *The Economics of Legal Minimum Wages*, American Enterprise Institute, Washington DC, 1981.

[7] J. P. Martin: 'The effects of the minimum wage on the youth labour market in North America and France,' *OECD Occasional Studies*, OECD, Paris, 1983.

[8] C. Brown, C. Gilroy and B. Kohen: 'The effect of minimum wages on employment and unemployment', in *Journal of Economic Literature*, 20, 1982, pp. 487–528.

[9] See Solon (1985), op. cit. and Wellington (1991), op. cit.

The freezing of the minimum wage during the Reagan presidency at USD 3.35 and its raising to USD 4.25 after the election of George Bush provided an almost experimental situation for testing the impact of the minimum wage on employment. According to previous estimates this increase of more than 25% should have reduced employment among young persons by at least 2%. However, the most recent studies detect no significant negative impact on employment, and some studies find that the minimum wage increase may actually have increased employment.[10] Whether this second generation of studies is more reliable than the what preceded it will require further examination as more data become available. A study which reconciled the two different sets of results by attributing one set to some form of misspecification, with the other emerging as more robust, would be extremely helpful.

(iv) Research on Europe: A First Generation of Studies

In many ways the experience of European countries is more interesting. Unlike the United States, European labour markets tend to be corporatist, with the majority of wages set through collective bargaining, and far more regulated. Those countries which have national minimum wages—France, the Netherlands, Portugal, Spain, Belgium and Luxembourg—take a very different approach to that of the US. Their coverage is generally complete with the implication that any employment effect will show up clearly there being no formal uncovered sector (as in the US) into which displaced workers can be absorbed. Furthermore, upratings are automatic and regular so that the minimum wage represents a constant constraint on enterprises.

The earliest studies examined the French experience. National minimum wages have existed there since 1950 and typically cover around 10% of workers. However, it appeared that the minimum wage had no effect on the youth labour market.[11] During the 1980s the minimum wage evolved by a series of discretionary (politically inspired) increases, which caused its value relative to average earnings to increase. Studies which used data for this period found a negative but small effect on the employment of workers aged under 25,[12] and suggested that an increase of 10% in the minimum wage reduced young persons' employment by 1 to 2%.

[10] R. B. Freeman: 'Minimum wages—again!', in *International Journal of Manpower*, 15, 1994, pp. 8–25.

[11] Martin, op. cit.

[12] G. Benhayoun: 'Salaire minimum et l'emploi des jeunes,' Centre d'Economic Regionale, University of Aix–Marseille·III, 1990. S. Bazen and J. P. Martin: 'The Impact of the Minimum Wage on the Earnings and Employment of Young People and Adults in France 1963–85', in *OECD Economic Studies*, 16, 1991, pp. 199–221. G. Ducos and J.M. Plassard: 'Salaire minimum et demande de travail des jeunes,' paper presented at SESAME, Clermont Ferrand, 1991. N. Skourias: 'Salaire minimum et emploi des jeunes: l'experience francaise,' paper presented at the international Conference on the Economics of Low Pay and the Effects of Minimum Wages, Arles, France, 1993.

The only other existing studies concern the Netherlands, Portugal and Greece. Minimum wages are found to reduce youth and adult employment in the Netherlands but the size of the effect is less clear. In a series of studies by van Soest different elasticity estimates have been calculated—the most recent being of the order of a 5 to 6% reduction in the employment of young persons for a 10% rise in the minimum wage, and a slightly lower figure for adults.[13] Earlier estimates were larger and differences can be traced to the data sources used and, to some extent, to difficulties in separating the different causes of unemployment. In Portugal, preliminary findings suggest that the minimum wage has had a negative impact on young persons' employment, particularly that of young women.[14] In contrast with other studies the impact is larger for 20 to 24 year olds (an elasticity of − 0.47) than for teenagers (− 0.2). For Greece, where minimum wage rates are set by national level collective agreements and are legally binding on all employers, one study finds that employment in manufacturing industry is reduced by 1% for a 10% increase in the minimum wage.[15]

The evidence that exists for European countries points therefore to a negative impact on employment mainly affecting young persons. Whether this research will come to be characterised as 'first generation' and undermined by further studies remains to be seen—the availability of data for this kind of study has hitherto been limited (many of the studies cited use annual data for periods of less than 25 years). Already some doubts are being expressed about the extent of the impact of the minimum wage in France. The youth employment series has recently been revised on the basis of population census data and a recast study finds the effect of the minimum wage to be far less significant than previous studies have suggested.[16]

4. Conclusion

In view of the different results obtained for different studies in different countries it is difficult to draw firm conclusions as to the direction and size of the impact of minimum wages on employment. The American consensus

---

[13] A. van Soest: 'Youth minimum wage rates: the Dutch experience,' in *International Journal of Manpower*, 15, 1994, pp. 101–117.

[14] M. E. Ribeiro: 'Le salaire minimum au Portugal: les incidences sur l'emploi', paper presented at the International Conference on the Economics of Low Pay and the Effects of Minimum Wages, Arles, France, 1993.

[15] V. Koutsogeorgopoulou: 'The impact of minimum wages on industrial wages and employment in Greece', in *International Journal of Manpower*, 15, 1994, pp. 86–100.

[16] G. Benhayoun: 'The impact of minimum wages on youth employment revisited: a note on the robustness of the relationship', in *International Journal of Manpower*, 15, 1994, pp. 82–85.

of the early 1980s has been undermined by recent studies and in Great Britain it is difficult to find evidence sufficiently robust to justify abolition of the Wages Councils.[17]   There does, however, appear to be a difference between the employment impact of minimum wages in the European countries which have full coverage and regularly uprated national minimum wages (France, the Netherlands, Portugal and Greece) and those with limited coverage (the United States and Great Britain.) This may, however, be due to the fact that research is more advanced in some countries than in others, particularly because of the limited number of data sets and the predominantly time series nature of the data used. What seems to have emerged so far, however, is that in some countries there are doubts concerning the existence of a minimum wage effect on employment and where an impact is found, its extent is small and largely confined to young persons.

These conclusions are drawn from the experience of a number of industrialised countries in which minimum wages have operated for a long time. Nevertheless, there are lessons that can be drawn for the design of minimum wage fixing arrangements in Central and Eastern European countries, especially as regards coverage, uprating and minimum wage levels. While minimum wages should be uniform across sectors in order to provide effective protection, there may be a case for different treatment of the agricultural sector in view of non–wage components in remuneration. Furthermore, minimum wage fixing bodies should study the advantages and disadvantages of fixing lower rates for young persons. Lacking experience and often requiring on–the–job training, lower minimum wage rates can be justified, perhaps a 10 to 20% reduction in the adult minimum rate during training. However, the period for which the lower rate can be paid if no training is provided should probably be limited, as in the United States where the sub–minimum rate is payable only for the first six months. The coverage of minimum wage fixing arrangements may be also modified in respect of regions between which the cost of living can vary greatly. Such a measure might also serve to eliminate regional imbalances as enterprises move to areas where the minimum wage is lower thereby promoting employment and growth.

As far as uprating is concerned, it would be wise to avoid the US system in which each uprating must be debated by Congress, which makes minimum wage increases rather irregular. Far preferable is the indexation of minimum wages to the cost of living; the difficulty here relates to the timing of minimum wage increases in order to maintain its real value. In France

[17] S. Machin and A. Manning: 'Minimum wages, wage dispersion and employment: Evidence from the UK Wages Councils', University College London, Discussion Papers in Economics, No. 92–05, 1992.

the indexation mechanism is triggered whenever retail prices increase by 2%—in inflationary periods this can result in five or more upratings in a single year. In Central and Eastern European countries it may be preferable either to uprate the minimum wage once a year to take into account the annual rate of inflation or to use a higher trigger value of 5%. Furthermore, in order to avoid social tensions over this issue it may be expedient to link the uprating of the minimum wage to improvements in productivity, so ensuring that the low paid also benefit from economic growth.

In France for example the minimum wage must increase annually by at least half the growth in real average manual earnings.

Finally, there is the question of the level of the minimum wage. If set too low, as in the United States, productivity growth may be hindered for efficiency wage reasons. If set too high, minimum wages limit scope for wage differentials based on skill and 'human capital' differences. This could also lead to lower skill levels and lower productivity. Furthermore, too high a minimum wage could exacerbate inflationary pressures and necessitate a tightening of macroeconomic policy with negative effects on employment. At the same time, if a minimum wage is set too high relative to general wage levels the development of appropriate collective bargaining arrangements is likely to be hindered.

SINCE THE LATE 1980s incomes have fallen sharply in most countries of Central and Eastern Europe, with unemployment and poverty rates rising dramatically. The statutory minimum wage was intended to act as an anchor of the social protection system in these countries, shielding the low-paid and those dependent on state benefits. Unfortunately, in recent years the minimum wage has dropped well below the subsistence level and has effectively ceased to offer any protection to those in need, becoming instead a means of impoverishment and destitution.

The ILO's Central and Eastern European Team has conducted a series of studies concerning the role of minimum wages in the countries of this rapidly transforming region, in particular looking at ways in which this role should be revised. Based on this research, *Minimum Wages in Central and Eastern Europe* examines the most crucial issues in Bulgaria, the Czech Republic, Hungary, Moldavia, Poland, Romania and Russia, and compares their systems with those of western industrialized economies. Bringing together primary data so far unknown beyond a small circle of policymakers and officials, the contributors consider the evidence and the implications of new developments and recommend a series of reforms.

About the editors

Guy Standing is currently Director of Labour Market Policies for the International Labour Office in Geneva, and until late 1994 was director of the ILO's Central and Eastern European Team in Budapest. He has been co-chairman of the Basic Income European Network since 1988.
Daniel Vaughan-Whitehead worked for the European Commission and joined the ILO in 1991. He is now Senior Wages Specialist for the ILO's Central and Eastern European Team.

Contributors: Stephen Bazen, IERSO, University of Bordeaux, France; **Gilbert Benhayoun**, University of Aix-Marseille, France; **Alena Buchtikova**, Czech National Bank; **Tatyana Chetvernina**, Centre for Labour Market Studies, Institute of Economics, Russian Academy of Sciences; **Krzysztof Hagemejer**, Social Security Department, ILO, Geneva; **Jenő Koltay**, Institute of Economics, Hungarian Academy of Sciences; **Steliana Pert**, Romanian Institute of Economics; **Nicolae Popescu**, Wage Department, Romanian Ministry of Labour; **Valentina Postolachi**, Federation of Independent Trade Unions of Moldavia; **Todor Radev**, Institute of Economics, Bulgarian Academy of Sciences; **Vasilira Rotaru**, Centre for Studies on Market Problems, Moldavian Academy of Sciences; and **Vassile Stoianov**, Centre for Studies on Market Problems, Moldavian Academy of Sciences.

Also published by CEU Press in association with ILO-CEET:
The Ukrainian Challenge: reforming labour market and social policy

**Central European University Press
in association with
International Labour Office
Central and Eastern Europe**

ISBN 1-85866-043-2

9 781858 660431